HOW TO MAKE ONE HELL OF A PROFIT AND STILL GET TO HEAVEN

Also by Dr. John F. Demartini

The Breakthrough Experience
Count Your Blessings
The Heart of Love
The Riches Within
You Can Have an Amazing Life. . . in Just 60 days!

HAY HOUSE TITLES OF RELATED INTEREST

The Abundance Book, by John Randolph Price

Attitude Is Everything for Success:
Say It, Believe It, Receive It, by Keith D. Harrell

How to Ruin Your Financial Life, by Ben Stein

Money Cards, by Suze Orman

The Power of Intention, by Dr. Wayne W. Dyer

Suze Orman's Protection Portfolio

10 Secrets for Success and Inner Peace, by Dr. Wayne W. Dyer

Yes, You Can Be a Successful Income Investor:
Reaching for Yield in Today's Market,
by Ben Stein and Phil DeMuth

All of the above are available at your local bookstore,
or may be ordered by visiting:

Hay House USA: **www.hayhouse.com**®
Hay House Australia: **www.hayhouse.com.au**
Hay House UK: **www.hayhouse.co.uk**
Hay House South Africa: **www.hayhouse.co.za**
Hay House India: **www.hayhouse.co.in**

HOW TO MAKE ONE
HELL OF A
PROFIT
AND STILL GET TO
HEAVEN

Dr. John F. Demartini

HAY
HOUSE

HAY HOUSE, INC.
Carlsbad, California • New York City
London • Sydney • Johannesburg
Vancouver • Hong Kong • New Delhi

Published and distributed in the United States by: Hay House, Inc.: www.hayhouse.com • *Published and distributed in Australia by:* Hay House Australia Pty. Ltd.: www. hayhouse.com.au • *Published and distributed in the United Kingdom by:* Hay House UK, Ltd.: www.hayhouse.co.uk • *Published and distributed in the Republic of South Africa by:* Hay House SA (Pty), Ltd.: www.hayhouse.co.za • *Distributed in Canada by:* Raincoast: www.raincoast.com • *Published in India by:* Hay House Publishers India: www.hayhouse.co.in

Editorial supervision: Jill Kramer • *Freelance project editor:* Gail Fink
Design: Amy Rose Grigoriou

Library of Congress Cataloging-in-Publication Data

Demartini, John F.
  How to make one hell of a profit and still get to heaven / John F. Demartini.
    p. cm.
  ISBN 1-4019-0198-0 (Tradepaper)
  1. Finance, Personal—Moral and ethical aspects. 2. Investments—Moral and ethical aspects. I. Title.
  HG179.D39 2004
  332.024'01—dc21

                                        2003008567

ISBN 978-1-4019-0198-1

16 15 14 13   12 11 10 9
1st printing, March 2004
9th printing, February 2013

FSC
www.fsc.org
MIX
Paper from
responsible sources
FSC® C011935

Printed in the United States of America

This book is dedicated to:

*Those wise souls who would love to expand
and integrate their spiritual and material wealth
through love and gratitude.*

Contents

Foreword

MY FRIEND Dr. John Demartini is a money-master. He has extensively and intensively experienced, mastered, and wisely teaches the laws of money. John is a genius who loves to share his expertise in an easy-to-understand, absorbing, easily assimilated, and useful way.

If you're ready for the art, science, and philosophy of money mastery to become the truth of your experience and expression, drink deeply of the wisdom in this cherishable book.

As co-author of the bestselling book, *The One Minute Millionaire: The Enlightened Way to Wealth,* I can guarantee John's techniques, ideas, insights, and challenges. He'll take you to your next level of financial success, prosperity, and abundance. He'll make your journey one of effortless effort, joy, and absolute fulfillment.

Dr. Demartini is one of the all-time great and inspiring teachers, speakers, writers, and leaders. I love learning from this wise man who is becoming cosmically conscious. As I've introduced my partners, like Jack Canfield, and friends at my seminars and rallies to John, all want to sit at his feet like Plato did Socrates.

John's mind and inspired thinking always stand the proverbial test of time. His big, audacious goal is to have one billion students who will positively and effectively impact the world. I believe, know, and see him doing it.

You're holding in your hands a book that will positively change your life, your future, and our world in an omni-beneficial way. Read it, reread it, take ownership of its priceless principles and philosophy, and become free economically and spiritually. Share it with others so they can do the same or more.

I believe this book will elevate you to a heavenly state of mind. Heaven is an inside-out job. When you find heaven within, it will manifest, like it has for John and me, in your every outward experience. Your eyes will sparkle. Your countenance will be radiant. You'll be passionately on-purpose. You'll make a difference and leave a legacy of significance.

I congratulate you in advance for creating an infinitely better future by absorbing these great truths.

— **Mark Victor Hansen**
Co-creator of the #1 *New York Times* bestselling series
Chicken Soup for the Soul® and co-author of
The One Minute Millionaire

Introduction

YOU MIGHT very well ask why someone would write a book entitled *How to Make One Hell of a Profit and Still Get to Heaven.* The answer is simple: Although millions of people worldwide dream of making a good living, attaining great wealth, and living extraordinary and fortunate lives, they fear that it can only be done at the expense of others or by compromising their higher spiritual values and virtuous nature. In other words, they don't believe that they can make a profit and still get into heaven!

Some people outwardly acknowledge their desire for great wealth but feel inwardly guilty about acquiring it. Many of these same people imagine that in acquiring wealth they'll somehow become evil, as if the "devil" will get them if they make profits, or God won't love them unless they're poor. This inner conflict between "heavenly" good and "hellish" profit stunts their growth in both spiritual and material matters, creating an almost incapacitating poverty complex that blocks future opportunities and fortunes.

Other people say that they just want to be comfortable and secure rather than vastly fortunate. This kind of thinking not only keeps them from breaking through to new levels of financial freedom, but it also holds them back from living their most cherished and inspiring dreams.

In addition to conflicts between their spiritual and material natures, some people have an internal struggle between their desires to give and to receive. They wish to be spiritually altruistic and care for others by giving, yet they have an equal and opposite desire to be materialistically narcissistic and care for themselves by receiving. Deep inside, these people believe that it's better to give to others than to themselves. They have yet to learn how to integrate the two sides into one balanced whole that would enable them to build solid financial foundations. Just as a nation's economy needs both supply and demand sides to function, so too must individuals learn to give *and* receive. When the two are brought consciously into balance, they unleash exceptional power.

By shedding light on an entirely new way of looking at, understanding, and appreciating the true nature of earthly profits and heavenly wealth, *How to Make One Hell of a Profit and Still Get to Heaven* can assist you in making your financial dreams come true.

This book is designed to wake you up to the true nature of wealth and fulfillment. It will teach you to think and care about money, to respect and understand it, and to address the many beliefs that may be interfering with your right and destiny to have it. This book will enlighten and immerse you in wealth from so many different angles and levels that it will pervade your consciousness and you'll begin to *resonate* with it—you'll actually become a money magnet. The fact that you're reading this book means you have the desire, and what I offer is the knowledge and practical skills to achieve greater financial freedom. So let's do it together.

If you read and apply the principles and methodologies laid out in these pages, you'll discover that while making profits obviously implies the receiving side of the economic equation, increasing them requires giving the gift of loving, grateful, value-added service. In the pages of this book, you'll learn how to tap in to one of the greatest of all spiritual, material, and financial laws: the principle of fair exchange, which means paying a reasonable price for a satisfactory service in a timely manner. Giving and receiving are two of the grandest expressions of life, and fair exchange is one of the keys to experiencing a heightened level of fulfillment beyond your greatest dreams.

You'll also learn some simple but profound principles that will impact your spiritual and financial life immeasurably, including these:

Payment is due when service is rendered.

Profits are a by-product of loving services rendered.

I invite you to come on a journey with me and explore the true nature of heavenly wealth and service, where genuine love and appreciation for the blessings of life occur. This journey will introduce you to a world that is not only beautiful, but one that overflows with magnificence and poise. Your body, mind, and soul are about to experience something unique—a whole new paradigm in financial thinking and feeling. With a little willingness and courage, you can receive even more of what a wealthy life has to offer and be able to give even more of what you have in exchange. There truly is a *financial heaven,* and it's available right here, right now.

If you'll join me on this journey, your relationship with and ability to master your spiritual wealth and material finances, as well as other vital areas of your life, will undergo an amazing transformation, and that's my intention for you.

Thank you, and welcome to the world of greater profits and heavenly riches.

— **Dr. John F. Demartini**

Chapter One

What the Hell Is Heaven?

*"A feast is made for laughter, and wine maketh merry:
but money answereth all things."*

— Ecclesiastes 10:19

LIKE ALL great quests, the search for spiritual and financial wealth begins with a question: So what the hell does heaven have to do with wealth? Let's find out.

For the purposes of this book, *heaven* represents a heartfelt state of appreciation, fulfillment, and presence—which means being in the here-and-now, not in the future with imagined fear or in the past with remembered guilt. This heartfelt state arises from a perception of balance, harmony, and order. When you know that everything around and within you is in a state of order, you feel grateful and fulfilled. You think and act with grace and poise, and you live with love and appreciation. This is a powerfully creative and *magnetic* state in which to be. In this state, you feel profoundly different within yourself, and others feel that difference, too.

You draw entirely different circumstances and opportunities into your life, including greater financial abundance.

Gratitude for the blessings of life awakens a deep sense of worthiness, belonging, and knowing that you have a special and meaningful mission to fulfill. As you grow in appreciation and love, you trust yourself and this underlying order, and your latent talents spontaneously begin to blossom. In fact, it's only a perceived lack of self-love that keeps them hidden, like the flowers of an unwatered garden.

Heaven, then, is this state of uplifted and enlightened spirit. A heavenly state occurs whenever you acknowledge that life's underlying magnificence and order is available everywhere and any time, no matter what the apparent circumstances. You or any individual or company that understands this will inevitably prosper.

Conversely, whenever you perceive that your life is filled with chaos, you experience nonfulfillment and you feel powerless. At such times, you repel people and opportunities, you imagine that you are struggling in "hell," and you react with what I call dis-grace (which not only means to be out of favor, dishonored, or shamed, but also includes not being grateful, inspired, or in communion with divinity because of judgment, distortion, misperception, or misinterpretation). In such moments, you even say things like, "Man, living like this is just hell!"

Defined this way, both heaven and hell are states of *mind,* one ordered and the other disordered. But here's the most exciting part of all: You have the ability to choose which of these states you would love to live in.

One of the great secrets of the universe is that everything is in perfect order already, and the only thing keeping you out of heaven, with all of its spiritual and material bounties, is a lack of awareness and appreciation of that divine order. However, when you appreciate your life, your life actually increases or *appreciates* in value, and your self-worth and self-love grow. Through such appreciation, your station in life is automatically elevated.

Everything Is Light

I was at a dinner party in New York a few years ago when, during a conversation about spirituality, the question of God came up. I turned to a noted Cambridge professor of physics seated to my left and asked him, "What do *you* think God is?"

He replied, "From all our studies, the best description we have of God is light. Light is the most probable and plausible essential substance we have found to describe the nature of God."

I then asked him, "So how would you describe human consciousness?"

"Most likely as a by-product of light."

Almost every spiritual teaching acknowledging God would agree with the physics professor that the inherent nature of divinity is love and light. Spirit is light, and it permeates every level of material existence.

Since both science and religion seem to agree that God is light, could we be emanations from such a loving Source? I define God to be the Grand Organized Design (or Designer) of a universe filled with heavenly light. What scientist, theologian, or layperson can look at the cosmos and not see a magnificently ordered design bursting with light?

Viewed from the spiritual and material perspectives, *light* has two meanings—in its spiritual essence it means purity or radiance, and in its material expression it refers to density or weight— but both spirit and matter ultimately consist of light. Light is the essence underlying our existence. The universe is full of radiant light, which is, in essence, love. The more light you have, the more love, gratitude, and order you have in your life. The more you experience this divinity, the more worthy you feel and the more you receive its spiritual and material blessings. If you're not so sure about that, just stay with me.

Some people make arbitrary distinctions between spirit and matter, but I ask, Where is God or spirit not? You may see someone meditating or praying and think, *That's a spiritual activity,* and then see someone else exchanging money to make a purchase and think, *Well, that's obviously material.* And yet the meditator may be praying for personal gain, while the shopper may be joyously buying a gift for a loved one. If you knew what was really occurring, you might completely reverse your first opinions.

If you deeply investigate what you call material actions, you might find that they're spiritual in essence. If you investigate what you think of as spiritual, you may discover that it involves matter. Spirit requires matter to express itself, and matter needs spirit to give it motion and meaning. As your understanding grows, you begin to see spirit and matter in all things, as two inseparable aspects of the same divine root substance that we call by many names: light, love, spirit, or even energy.

Actually, this universe may be nothing more than light at many different frequencies. Energy manifests itself in the form of waves and particles, which, in their essence, are nothing but light. Some physicists even say that matter is simply dense or low-frequency light. To our physical senses, the higher frequencies of light appear to be pure spirit, and the lower frequencies seem to be only matter, but in reality, spirit and matter are inextricably linked in a loving, cosmic dance at all frequencies. In your investigations of spirit and matter, the questions you ask determine which of the two you can see, and the wisest questions reveal both. When you see the two as an ordered one, your love, self-worth, and wealth will grow.

The Ultimate Secret to Wealth and Fulfillment

Your wealth and fulfillment in life are expressions of your heart, mind, and soul. The more the latter are awakened, the more the former may be elevated. There's a widespread spiritual and business belief that formless spirit and form-full matter are somehow different, or even opposites, but as stated previously, this distinction is an illusion. There is no existence without a perfect combination of the two; in fact, they're not even two, they're *one.* Therefore, you'd be wise to make your spiritual life a business and your business life a spiritual experience. In other words, incorporate your heart, mind, and soul into your business. Put your *spirit* into your work. Pour on your inspiration. The most fulfilled people I've met are the ones who are inspired. They act like missionaries for their work. They put their spirit and inspiration into their interactions with those they meet, and they receive magnificent rewards in return.

You'd be wise to remember that, just as you are light, all matter *including money* is ultimately light. In fact, the word *gold* comes from the Hebrew *aour,* which means "light." The only things keeping you and money apart are the limiting beliefs you hold about it.

Love and appreciation are powerful magnetic forces. If you don't know how to love and appreciate wealth, if you unconsciously resist and mistrust it by misunderstanding its true nature, why would it be drawn to you? But when you transcend any limiting illusions about wealth and embrace it as a manifestation of spirit-matter, it walks right up and offers itself to you. You either attract abundance into your life or you keep it away, depending on how you think and feel. When spirit (cause) and matter (effect) come equally and fully together in your consciousness, heaven is born. If you would love to get to heaven, you would be wise to learn how to love and appreciate spiritual matter, including its earthly form called wealth.

Spirit Really Matters

The two great social forces, or two aspects of life, that move masses of people or cultures more than anything else in this world are spiritual wealth and material wealth. These are two of the highest motivating forces within the human psyche. They motivate and fulfill our immortal and mortal natures. Whenever or wherever these two forces come together, tremendous power is unleashed.

Within the school I founded, called the Concourse of Wisdom School of Philosophy and Healing, I present many different courses, but an idea common to them all is this interconnectedness of spirit and matter. Some years ago, a woman who desired to attend one of my courses approached me. She asked me why I charged a fee for my educational and inspirational services. I provided her with various answers, including information about my research time, an explanation of how her paying would contribute to her appreciation and application, and a few words about the importance of putting a value on one's service, but nothing seemed to satisfy her questioning.

Finally, I recited the wise old proverb, "When service is rendered, payment is due," and then I explained, "If you attend the program, it's certainly fair that you *pay* something." So she came, and she paid, yet she still didn't understand.

During the course, she came up to me and asked yet again, "Dr. Demartini, *why* do you want to charge money for your services?" She was still stuck on this question.

So I said to her, "The people who generally ask me this question are often the ones with 'poverty complexes.' They're confused about the purpose and value of money. The wealthy often tell me I would be wise to charge a lot *more* for my services. Although being wealthy isn't necessarily the answer to everything, it certainly offers us more life-fulfilling opportunities than downright poverty does. Prosperity and progression often rise together, while poverty and regression often walk hand in hand."

As I spoke with her, I could see that the perception of a lack of money was running this woman's life, so I asked her, "Where did you get the idea that services are better given freely, or that a lack of money is somehow better and more spiritual than an abundance of it?"

"I guess from my Christian spiritual teachings."

"Do you realize that some religious institutions have the greatest financial wealth on the face of the earth, yet they're also the source of the very idea that it's more blessed to give *to* them than to receive *from* them? Could this be a form of marketing and a way to fill their coffers so as to maintain their existence?"

She said, "Well, that's a good point."

I continued, "The great world religions have also associated at some point in time with military power and fantastic wealth. If you want your church to make a difference, it will require both spiritual warriors and monetary wealth. If you have neither within your church, don't count on it growing."

"You know, that's one of our concerns," she agreed. "We only have 275 members, and our size never seems to increase."

Speaking candidly, I said, "That may be because you're minimizing one of the great spiritual powers—wealth—and few will desire to join and invest in your spiritual cause until *you* learn to appreciate and invest in it. This holds for you individually, too. Few are going to join *with* you and financially invest *in* you until you invest in yourself."

By the end of the course, she finally began to understand the importance of money and how wise money management could assist her church. Since she's begun emphasizing the importance of material wealth in building her church, her church has started to grow. Unfortunately, although she sees the value of money in growing her church, she hasn't completely comprehended the significance of this message for herself. Apparently that's still too big of a jump for her.

What you believe and what you say to yourself manifests in your life. When people believe the incomplete teaching that money isn't spiritual, it's no wonder they don't have any significant degree of monetary wealth. They creatively manifest exactly what they have decided to believe and value. Yet the same religious institutions that put forward such an incomplete teaching hold some of the greatest reservoirs of monetary wealth in the world. Within that apparent contradiction is a profound message about the true nature of spirituality: It is not and never truly has been separate from material matters, except in certain unaware minds. Any great spiritual teacher who has ever had a powerful spiritual message to communicate to the planet—from the Buddha to Jesus to Mohammed to the Dalai Lama—inevitably required or associated with wealth in order to spread his message. That's how it works.

One night my wife, Athena, and I joined Robin Leach, host of the television show *Lifestyles of the Rich and Famous,* for a late dinner at Elaine's, a popular New York restaurant. During our conversation, Robin described the filming of his second program,

Treasures of the Vatican. He told us that while doing research for the show, he'd been given access to what he termed "the underground city of wealth," a city existing deep within the chambers and chapels beneath and around Italy's holy Vatican. He estimated that if the vast riches sitting in those chambers, chapels, and vaults were distributed equally among the world's six billion people— all the gold, diamonds, emeralds, jewels, statues, paintings, and frescoes—every person on the planet would become vastly fortunate indeed. Obviously, the Catholic Church understands the value of wealth or money.

The religions of the world perform a great service by striving to communicate various messages about the spiritual realms, but they wouldn't have gotten off the ground without material wealth. How else could they have built the great temples, synagogues, mosques, and cathedrals, and filled them with works of the creative human spirit? They wisely acquired the finest writings, paintings, sculptures, music, and architecture to attract and inspire. Without that power and beauty, their message might have been lost. Matter must have spirit if it is to *move* us, but spirit requires matter in order to *express* itself. Matter is like the effect, while spirit is like the cause.

To Be Is to Do Is to Have

If you want to make a spiritual difference and do a tremendous material service for the world, you're going to be faced with the other side of the equation, where receiving and having abundance reside. In other words, *to be is to do is to have.*

As strange as it may seem, the more you rise up in spirit or grace, the more power you'll have to manifest wealth. Intangible spirit and tangible matter are like the two sides of a golden coin, and if you reject either side you don't get to keep the richness of such gold.

As you've already learned, one of the great secrets of manifesting prosperity is to simply love and appreciate your life. It may seem harder to be grateful for life when you long for beauty, possessions, and experiences you think you can't have, and for gifts you desire, yet feel you can't give to yourself. That produces an ungrateful state, or "endarkenment" of spirit, a sense of being in dis-grace, and it's a powerful wealth repellent that will persist until you wake up to the indivisibility of spirit and matter and learn to embrace and appreciate both equally.

It's revitalizing and wise to allow yourself to be, do, and have the things you love. It's your divine birthright. I often meet people who say, "No, I've risen above such superficial desires or petty needs. I only think in terms of spirituality. I don't judge people by their material possessions or achievements. I just look at the quality or essence of the person, not their existence." But if a highly accomplished person who does and has a lot approaches them, one who radiates great confidence about who he or she is in the world, you can watch these same people literally shrink and withdraw from the high achiever because of their own relatively diminished self-worth. They put *themselves* down because they feel less than they could be in comparison. Because they haven't yet discovered where they're giving and receiving, they feel less worthy. But deep inside their heart, they know that all is spiritual matter, and it's all worthy of respect or honor.

There actually exists a state of equilibrium. You receive in exact proportion to the value you give. Therefore, what you do and what you have definitely say a lot about who you *are.* If you have many clients and enterprises and huge resources and give a great deal of service to the world, you're seen as an important person. But if you do nothing and have nothing, society around the world will label you as being a "nobody." The many lopsided religious ideals concerning money are often the source of such diminished human feelings. Wise or unwise, that's the nature of humanity, and if you're honest, you'll admit that you feel the same way about yourself.

There's a model in psychology that says nothing matters but your *being*—who you are—and it has nothing to do with what you do or have. That model is misguided idealism. If you put someone in a state of just "being" by taking away all their "doings" and "havings," you'll see that as they fall in society, they'll also descend in self-image and self-worth. As long as you're alive in your body, you can't separate the three aspects of being, doing, and having. If you don't *have* anything and don't *do* anything, you'll be unable to avoid feeling less worthy. That's because your service to the world (production) and what you're willing to receive for it (compensation) combine to make up who you are. Life is designed to make sure you express your unique talents and find fulfillment.

The Power of Words

What you do influences what you have, but what you *say* has a big influence on what you'll allow yourself to do. What might happen if you talked to yourself differently? How would you *love* to talk to yourself?

I once worked with a classical guitarist who had just enough money to get by from day to day, and he thought it was somehow noble to be a "starving artist." He came to a class I was giving on goal setting, and afterward he asked me, "Will you be my mentor?"

I said, "Yes, but I ask that you do something for me in return, for it's unwise to do something for nothing." In return for my mentoring, he came to my office and played the most magnificent music.

One day I said to him, "I know you love music, but if you continue to play without rewarding yourself, your love for playing music could wane. From now on, your conversation with yourself about being a 'starving artist' is not to dominate your life." I had him begin saying, "I am a highly paid professional musician." You may laugh at that, because it seems so simple, but he began saying to himself, "I am a highly paid professional musician. Whenever I perform, I receive new creative ideas on how to become even more handsomely paid."

About three weeks later he said to me, "An idea came to me last night while I was playing. I'll record my upcoming performance with the symphony orchestra and sell the tapes at the end of my shows. Nobody seems to be doing it, but I'm going to try anyway and see what happens."

The very first night, 75 people paid $10 each for his tape. He said, "It was amazing. No one had the courage to do this before, but I just broke through my psychological barrier because I decided to be rewarded for my musical talent and art."

Most people ask themselves, "How can I afford to do this?" It's much wiser to ask, "How can I become wonderfully paid to do what I really love?" Ask a different question and you'll receive a very different answer to the same apparent situation.

That young man now performs in Europe and all over the United States. He has played at Carnegie Hall, at many other great venues, and with some of the major philharmonic orchestras in the country. Today he's a noted soloist who has published CDs, tapes, and books. He has more certainty, recognition, and opportunities, as well as a great deal more money and fame. He's playing more powerfully than ever and loving it even more, and it all happened for him when he gave up the belief and affirmation, *I am a starving artist.* You'd have a hard time convincing him he's a starving artist now—he doesn't say that anymore.

Now, besides repeating his original affirmation, "I am a highly paid professional musician," he also says to himself, "I am one of the great classical guitarists. When I play, even the birds and animals stop to listen." That man is certainly *inspired,* and it comes through in his music. He definitely touches people. You're not on this earth just to get by or survive. You're here to realize your grandest dreams. You have many more magnificent ambitions inside you still left to fulfill, some that are eager to pour forth. The more you're willing to act on them, the more you become of service to yourself and others, the greater your self-worth, and the more you'll spontaneously receive what you would love. When you're more willing to share your talents, inspirations, and *gifts* with the world, the desired gifts you receive in return will be even more abundant. Likewise, when you're willing to receive rewards for your efforts, you'll be less likely to lose heart and motivation for doing what you love. The more you're willing to receive, the more you'll be willing to give. You can't escape the two sides of doing and having, giving and receiving, in order to be.

*"If man knew that he himself was God and heaven and hell,
no illusions would have a hold on him; nothing
could limit his consciousness."*

— Daniel Odier, Tantric master

Master Mind

We all have a mission, a dream we would love to fulfill, and the greater that dream, the more resources it will magnetically attract to be fulfilled. One of the great keys that will unlock the door to your dreams and wealth is mastering your own mind, the source of all of your inner experiences of heaven and hell.

Heaven and hell are mental states of gratitude and ingratitude respectively, so mastering your mind becomes the key to entering the realm of spiritual as well as material wealth and well-being. Deep in many people's psyches is the idea that to be wealthy is to not be spiritual. It's a myth that keeps many people in poverty. When the majority of people are in poverty or a state of financial powerlessness, they're easily ruled by the few with wealth. When you feel powerless, it's hard to love yourself or your life, and doesn't that impact your spirit? It's a blessing to be able to expand your giving *and* receiving. To embrace both is to come into alignment with the laws of psychology, physics, wealth, and life itself, thus building your self-worth. That's the beginning of real financial power.

Developing wealth is vital to the growth of individuals, companies, and entire nations or cultures. Nowhere in the history of the earth has there been great culture, great art, great music, great architecture, great inspirational creations, or great intelligent minds without their being associated with wealth. Poverty doesn't lead to the highest expression of the human spirit, to the fulfillment of the vast potential within human beings. Without wealth, civilization stagnates. You can find poor cultures living today just as they did 2,000 or more years ago. Life seeks growth and change, and without ever-increasing financial resources, growth is slowed and stunted. The same principle applies to individuals.

You may still have some limiting beliefs in your mind, such as, "I'm not in it for the money," or "Money's not important to me," or phrases such as "filthy rich." Every time you repeat these types of statements to yourself or others, you throw thousands of dollars—possibly even *millions*—out of your pocket. Remember, what you believe and say to yourself manifests into reality. You create your own destiny with your thoughts every day.

There's a direct relationship between your ability to masterfully build financial wealth and your ability to fulfill your overall life potential. There are seven primary areas of life fulfillment—spiritual, mental, vocational, financial, social, familial, and physical. Any area that's not valued, honored, and more fully developed automatically becomes the weak or missing link in your fulfillment. Financial mastery is one of the most important, for it's a vital component in becoming all you can be.

Master your financial thoughts and you'll
master your financial destiny.

At the end of every chapter, you'll find one or two exercises similar to the ones that follow. I advise you to give yourself the opportunity of completing each of them before going on to the next chapter. If you work with them, they can work powerfully on you. Each exercise is designed to give you a personal experience of the principles set out in these pages, and the insights you'll gain are a vital part of the shift in consciousness that is the purpose of this book. I would also suggest that you purchase a notebook or journal that pleases you, and use it solely for these exercises.

After the exercises, you'll find a list of affirmations called Words of Wisdom and Power. Read them three times a day, ponder and meditate on their deeper meaning, see them in the world, and feel them in yourself as you go about your daily pursuits. They are profound principles concealed in simple words, and they can change the way you experience your financial life. Whenever you get a new insight, record it in your journal to remind you of your own financial growth and transformation.

Exercise 1

At the top of a journal page, make a list of everything that you consider an attribute of spirituality, such as *love, wisdom, freedom, generosity, healing, harmony, beauty, courage, light,* and *presence.* These are only a few possible examples; you'll have your own particular understanding and list of what *spiritual* means to you. Continue writing until you've listed everything you believe to be an aspect of spirituality.

Next, take each of your words, one at a time, and write down every single way that having great financial wealth will help you attain even more of that quality. Here's an example:

> *Freedom: I would no longer have to work for someone else, only for myself and with people I love. I would be able to travel the world and see the greatest and most inspiring natural beauty and human-made creations. I would have the freedom to do the things I told myself I would one day love to do, but never seemed to find the time for. I would be able to live anywhere I chose, in any state or country or climate, and move as often as I want; the entire planet would be my home. I would be free to buy the books, attend the classes, and see the artistic performances that would expand and inspire my mind. I would be free to learn and master any skill I chose.*

As you write, imagine how it would feel to actually live that way. *See* and *feel* what it would be like to travel, to have your own business and be your own boss, to gaze upon that beauty. Think in terms of all seven areas of life: spiritual, mental, vocational, financial, social, familial, and physical.

Imagine how much more grateful you can be for life when you can experience so much more of it. Don't stop until you feel a shift in your consciousness, until an enthusiasm for the power of building wealth arises in you and you know it's connected to your spiritual pursuits. When you can write it, see it, and feel it, you're more than halfway on the journey to creating it.

Exercise 2

Using the same spiritual attributes you listed for Exercise 1, go through each of them in turn and write down how a nonmastery or a *lack* of wealth limits your ability to express those same inspired qualities. This will prompt your mind to think from the other side, from experiences you may have already lived rather than those you would love to live. Here's an example:

> **Freedom:** *Without money, I would be unable to buy beautiful things for those I love. I would worry more about paying bills and doubt my own financial capabilities and worth. I would sometimes be stressed to such a degree that it would affect my health. I would experience financial fear and guilt. I would be unable to meet my financial obligations, so I would feel less confident and present. In this state of mind where a lack of wealth dominates, it would be hard to see and appreciate the hidden beauty and financial opportunities that surround me. I would think more about survival than I would about creativity, and this would generate desperation, the very antithesis of inspiration.*

This is a powerful tool for reversing any unexamined beliefs you may harbor about the spirituality of poverty, and it will open the doors of your mind to new possibilities of giving, receiving, and being.

Words of Wisdom and Power

- *My spirit without matter is expressionless, and my matter without spirit is motionless.*

- *Financial heaven is mine the moment I have a grateful heart and enlightened mind.*

- *My material wealth is another expression of my spiritual wealth.*

- *I am a master of my thoughts, and whatever I think about, I manifest or become.*

- *I am a money magnet, and I am vastly fortunate.*

- *I am a master of my financial thoughts. I am a master of my financial destiny.*

- *I embrace spirit and matter equally.*

Chapter Two

The Principle of Fair Exchange

"A man should make all he can, and give all he can."
— Nelson Rockefeller

IS IT more honorable to give or to receive? You might assume that it's more honorable to give, but that defies a basic law of nature involving the principle of fair exchange, which I define as paying a fair price for a fair service in a timely manner. Many people in their daily interactions with others would love to consciously maintain these types of dealings. However, even those with pure intentions frequently have difficulty accomplishing this. They often misunderstand what it really means to exchange fairly in the first place. They sometimes believe that they should be more generous to others than to themselves. But even the old cliché says: "Love thy neighbor *as* thyself." This means not more than, but equally.

To think it's more honorable to give than to receive is to break a profound universal law, the Law of Equilibrium, also known by modern science as the Law of Conservation or the Law of

Compensation. This law encompasses every energy event of life. From the quantum world within the atom to the atmosphere of human existence and out beyond the farthest galaxies, every energy exchange maintains a conservation or perfect balance between give and take. This grand law states that nothing is truly created or destroyed, nothing is ever gained or lost; everything is just transformed between different forms of energy. (The word *energy* here could also be termed *spirit*.) This law states that energy events involving exchange remain conserved throughout space-time.

Every time you try to step outside of this law and try to *receive* something for nothing, or try to *give* something for nothing, you oppose the very forces of nature and impede the growth of your self-worth. When you owe someone money or they owe you money, this seemingly unbalanced exchange takes you out of the present and places you into the elusive past or future. But how? Have you ever been behind on your payments to someone and felt guilty for being late, or were fearful about how you were going to pay them? Has anyone ever been behind on their payments to you, and you felt resentful, fearful, or guilty because you put yourself into such a precarious situation? The greater the perceived debt either way, the greater your mental distraction becomes, and the less empowered you and the other person are in such a relationship. This imbalance drags your mind out of the present and places it into the imagined future or remembered past. You may recall that earlier I defined *hell* as a powerless and distracted state involving fear and guilt about the future and past, while *heaven* is the resting state of gratitude balanced in the present.

Fair and Equitable Exchange

Maintaining fair exchange allows you to remain in the heavenly present. By bringing into balance acts of giving and receiving between yourself and others, you come into alignment with the conserving power of the universe, and magical things begin to happen. Let your giving and receiving get perceptually out of balance, and you work against the Law of Equilibrium, which will do everything it can to make sure you wake up to your illusions and steer you mentally back onto the balanced path of fulfillment.

Some people believe that in order to win or have their dreams fulfilled, someone else must lose. In contrast, there are those who believe that they must lose, sacrifice, or be diminished so that others might get ahead. Examples of these two polarities are found in the narcissists who exaggerate their self-importance and the altruists who exaggerate the importance of others. Perhaps you've occasionally thought of yourself as altruistic and found yourself giving more and more until you finally said, "The hell with this! I've been looking out for others and not receiving anything for myself." Then you went to the other extreme and said, "What's in it for me? I deserve more." Life has a way of eventually bringing these two misperceived extremes gradually back into balance. This is because the powerful present occurs right down the middle, the perfect balance between self-interest and interest in others. This is the key to fair exchange.

It's wise to give and receive fairly, equitably, and simultaneously. Maintaining fair exchange in daily dealings is one of the keys to having a quality life. The quality of your life is also based on the quality of your questions. So ask, "How can I give others what they would love while simultaneously receiving what *I* would love? How can I help fulfill both of us?" Ask yourself these questions daily and you'll be on your way to receiving an entirely new and more empowered financial life.

"The eye sleeps until the spirit awakens it with a question."

— James McKean

Pay Yourself First

When I started in business many years ago, I used to place myself last financially. I tried to be Mr. Nice Guy and make sure that all of my creditors and employees were paid first. At the end of the month, I would take whatever was left over, which wasn't much. I struggled financially, and even though I worked hard, long hours,

I always seemed to just break even. Meanwhile, my employees quit after only three months, six months, or sometimes a year. They'd come and go, while I still imagined their importance as somehow greater than my own. I was minimizing my contribution and exaggerating theirs.

Then one Monday morning, an employee whom I had been carefully putting first and paying first for almost a year, and who had suddenly gotten married over that prior weekend, gave me immediate notice. She expected her final pay and announced that she was quitting so she could move away. I suddenly woke up and said to myself, *Wait a minute now. Of all the people in my business, the most important or indispensable person presently is me. I'm the only one who stays no matter what, and I'm the one who puts in the most hours. The buck starts and stops with me, but I'm guaranteeing their salaries and not my own. That's just not smart, because I'm becoming less inspired about working here, and without me there's little or no business, and the remaining employees have no jobs.*

From that moment on, I turned things around. I made sure I was financially rewarded for my work, and I started paying myself first. That decision put the responsibility on my employees to make sure they produced, and then collected the money they deserved. From that very day, my financial foundation began to grow, and this strategy has worked ever since. I've made ever-increasing profits, my employees have greater job security and motivation, and they stay with me much longer. It's amazing—that one shift in emphasis created longer-lasting, more loyal and effective employees; increased capital and produced greater company stability; and both my employees and I grew more stable financially. Before that, I had it all reversed because my financial priorities were backward.

Some people might say, "Oh, that's so cold," but I'm just being honest. I'm willing to play out the roles of both cold and warm, whichever is effective, and now I have the ability to be generous with my employees while securing them so that when business inevitably fluctuates, they all still have jobs. Selfishness doesn't serve; enlightened self-interest does. Don't try to give more than you receive or you'll get a lesson to teach you that this approach is folly. Being able

to equally give *and* receive is a blessing. It's wise to receive as well
as to give, so start doing so and watch what happens.

There's No Such Thing As a Free Lunch

Some people lean toward the other side of the equation. They
look to get more than they give, but in the long run that doesn't
work or last either. The principle of fair exchange simply cannot
be ignored. Anytime you feel out of exchange in any of the
seven areas of life—spiritual, mental, vocational, financial, social,
familial, or physical—you waver from your state of presence and
generate fear and guilt. This will hold you back in each of those
areas until you perceptually return to equilibrium. The saying
"Payment is due when service is rendered" means that at the very
moment a service is rendered, payment must be made. That's one
of the secrets of being *present,* and it's an ancient secret that helps
build a powerful and wealthy consciousness. The universe is the
most enduring and ordered of all systems; it does not give or
receive something for nothing.

A lady once called me in to consult with her on an exciting
business proposition. She had recently become friends with a
successful businessman who offered her a $250,000 line of
credit to start a company, at no interest charges, to be paid back
whenever she liked. She was thrilled about it, but the moment
she asked my opinion I said, "Absolutely not!"

She was quite taken aback and said, "But . . . but what do
you mean? This is a fantastic deal! Why in the world shouldn't I
take it?"

"I know how it sounds," I said, "but I strongly advise you not
to do it without simultaneously structuring a clear, fair, and equitable exchange with this man. Getting 'something for nothing'
is not a formula for financial fulfillment. If you borrow this money,
make it very clear what you're going to pay and when—the
interest, time, and penalties, down to the last dollar. Don't leave
it open and hanging or you could disempower the relationship
you just made, and in all likelihood your business as well. You'll

almost certainly create unrealistic expectations and resentment, and disempower yourself in the process. Being rescued is unwise; being a fair and equal partner is wise." This woman was smart enough to take my advice, and their relationship has flourished both personally and financially.

How do you think investors feel when someone values them and has the integrity to make that kind of fair and equitable commitment in return? Confidence, trust, and respect are spontaneously created, generating many more opportunities in the future.

On the other hand, I recently worked with a man who lent a large sum of money to a desperate relative, and he'll probably never see this sum again. Because he didn't follow what I've just outlined, he'll almost certainly disrupt a family relationship and say good-bye to his hard-earned money. I can virtually guarantee that this transaction will result in disheartened feelings, because the two parties are so far out of fair exchange—unless, of course, the investor considers the lesson he learns as a fair lifelong compensation. His intention was to help or rescue, but he can't beat the spiritual laws of financial fair exchange.

Remember, these laws exist to teach you, and to firmly guide you back to the center path of fair exchange in every area of your life.

Balance the Heart

Of course, perceived debt is not limited to economics. Imbalances can show up with money, a gift or service, or even a romance. When imbalance occurs, the key is to find a way to get back into fair exchange. For example, I felt indebted to my parents for all the guidance and love they'd given me, so I wrote poems for them in a very appreciative and heartfelt state. In those verses, I thanked them for their great contribution to my life. My mother cried when she received hers. She had it framed and has kept it for many years, and I know that it was of immense value to her. She had given me so much, yet my gift was also special and was enough to her.

"They may forget what you said,
but they will never forget how you made them feel."

— Carl W. Buechner

People deeply desire to be recognized and acknowledged for what they've given, and it's such a simple thing to do if you just take the time. Fair exchange—receiving from someone and expressing your gratitude in return—has great power to move people. Expressions of gratitude can open up communication and cooperation with anyone in your life: Be it boss or employee, friend or neighbor, brother or sister, husband or wife, everyone responds to gratitude. This principle is so profound that it can bring people back into your life or let both of you move on.

Keeping your exchanges consciously balanced is a simple and powerful technique to increase both your material and mental value, but this principle can also work in reverse: You can sabotage hours, days, months, even years of your life by accumulating imbalanced exchanges. Dental studies, for example, have shown that people who don't pay their dentist bills have a much higher incidence of pain, filling dropouts, and broken teeth and bridges. They somehow sabotage their own teeth to justify themselves, because they have an inner obedience to this principle and feel guilty that they're out of fair exchange for the services they've received.

Accumulated imbalances hold you back by creating hidden agendas that keep you from being present. They generate distracting emotions and take up the space and time you could otherwise use to fulfill your life. But when you clear imbalances out of your mind by balancing them, you'll spontaneously be more present, certain, clear, and masterful.

Profit is not just a matter of finances, it's also about awakening clear *consciousness,* and every step you take toward one can increase the other. Have you ever thought you deserved more for work you've done but didn't ask for it, and felt somehow lessened and devalued afterward? When you do something for nothing, or for less than it's truly worth, you lower your self-worth and also rob the recipients of dignity and responsibility by making them feel consciously or unconsciously indebted to you. Likewise, you'll feel devalued if someone asks for less than they really deserve from you. Here's an example of how it works.

My friend Susan has another friend named Jill who owns a chain of beauty salons. Susan dropped by Jill's salon one day so she could have "the works," but she was charged far less than the service was worth. Jill was overvaluing Susan and undervaluing herself, and anytime you do that (or overvalue yourself and undervalue another), the world kicks in to try to teach you about such an illusion.

This had been going on for some time, and Susan was becoming so uncomfortable about getting special prices that she felt reluctant to go back. Realizing that she was feeling out of exchange and increasingly awkward around Jill, as an act of love Susan wisely said, "I love your salon, but I don't want a special deal anymore. I feel you're undervaluing your services, and I want to pay you what they're really worth." Susan instantly felt better about being in fair exchange, and so did Jill, because that's what she really desired but had been unwilling to request. The instant Jill was able to receive what she inwardly sensed her true value to be, her consciousness was cleared, and appreciation, deeper respect, and an even greater relationship emerged between the two friends. Speaking up in that way was a masterful act, because sometimes it takes real courage to talk about such matters. Deep inside, people appreciate it, and in their own time they'll understand and be grateful.

Certainty, love, appreciation, and presence arise the instant you have conscious fair exchange, and these are all qualities of self-mastery. Presence, in particular, is one of the great keys to mastery. You can't be present if you *give* something for nothing, or try to *receive* something for nothing. The way to maintain presence is through maintaining balance, and masterful people maintain it in as many aspects of their lives as possible. Be wise, caring, and courageous enough to maintain true fair exchange with those you love.

"Life shrinks or expands in proportion to one's courage."

— Anaïs Nin

I once met a great man named Foster Hibbard, who was a longtime student of Napoleon Hill, the author of *Think and Grow Rich*. Hibbard was a highly awakened man who taught universal financial principles most days of his adult life until well into his 70s. I had the opportunity to lecture with him before he passed away, and this is one of the lessons he gave me. He said, "Make a list of anything or anyone in your life that feels incomplete or out of balance, and find a way to bring it back into fair exchange. It will have an incredible effect on your mind and your finances."

Twelve-step programs, such as the one taught by Alcoholics Anonymous, use this principle to help people in crisis release their past by going back and making amends, but it's even more powerful when done on a daily basis. At the end of this chapter you'll find an exercise designed to help you get present in all your exchanges and begin transforming your life. Consciously reestablishing fair exchange is a freeing experience, and extraordinary things can happen when you do it.

The Ugly Duckling

Feeling out of balance can apply not just to other people, but also to your relationship with God or the whole world.

I once met a lady in Seattle who'd been born with vitiligo, a condition that made her skin look blotchy and multicolored. She was light pink, dark brown, and white all mixed together, and she looked like a patchwork quilt. Not only was her skin different, but she had an odd face with tiny ears and a kind of snout that made her look a little like a duck. The other kids in school wouldn't go near her; they called her the ugly duckling. Can you imagine being called that most days of your life? She's a lovely person inside, but she grew up feeling isolated, introverted, and ugly.

When she came to my Breakthrough Experience seminar (which is described more fully in my book *The Breakthrough Experience: A Revolutionary New Approach to Personal Transformation*), she participated in an exercise designed to help people find the balance and order in any event. Going through the exercise, she quickly uncovered the balance and order in the perceived affliction that seemed so unfair. She realized that because she had felt so ugly, she'd surrounded herself with beauty. Today she's one of the leading interior designers in the entire country, and she fills her whole life with beautiful things. I watched this lady, who had spent her childhood apparently mocked, ridiculed, and isolated, thank all the people who had called her "ugly duckling." One by one she went to each person in the room, saw every one of her perceived tormentors in them, and thanked them from her heart.

She said, "I had no idea God was working in my life at that time. I never dreamed He was giving me my destiny and guiding me to be someone great. What inspires me most is bringing beauty to this world and helping people see the beauty all around them. I have an innate ability to do that, and I want to thank you for helping me find it." She'd been told she was ugly, but now she's sought after all over America for the beauty she creates. When she saw the blessing, she didn't question the price.

If you feel you've paid a high price at some time in your life, find the blessing and return to your center.

Something for Something

Dr. Robert Schuller is a famous spiritual teacher, a wise and openhearted minister and founder of the Crystal Cathedral in Garden Grove, California. He became one of my mentors and shared a number of great spiritual principles with me. I first met him when I was 21 years old.

At that time, I was studying comparative religion and philosophy and was attending the University of Houston. During my winter vacation, I decided to experience a Christian revival retreat held in Boulder, Colorado. After the retreat was over, I figured that, since I was already halfway there, I would hitchhike to California and meet Dr. Schuller.

When I arrived, he was speaking to more than 400 executives in the cathedral, so I went to his office tower to make an appointment to meet him when his speech concluded.

Dressed in my slightly ragged and road-dusty clothes, and carrying my backpack, I walked across his crowded reception room and said to his secretary, "I'd like to meet Robert Schuller when he finishes his meeting."

She gave me a withering look over her glasses and said, "Young man, that's just not possible. He's a very busy man, and there are many gentlemen here who have made appointments months in advance. You'll have to submit a written application, and perhaps in a few months . . ."

I said, "You don't understand, ma'am. I hitchhiked all the way from Colorado, and I have to return to Texas tomorrow. I must see him. I'll do anything, even if it's just for a few minutes."

"Young man, I believe you heard me."

"All right. May I just sit here?"

"As long as you don't disturb these gentlemen."

About 30 minutes later, Robert Schuller's office door opened and there he was in the doorway, so I just hurried over and stood right next to him. The moment he said good-bye to the man he'd been talking to, he turned to me, took my hand, and said, "Hello, young man. Come right in." Amazing things can happen if you're clear and determined about what you want. All sorts of obstacles can simply evaporate before a powerful intention.

As I walked in, I glanced back at his secretary, and she was stunned—her glasses almost fell off her face. The other gentlemen in the waiting room looked at each other as if to say, *What the hell? Did you see that?* And then I proceeded to spend 45 minutes with Robert Schuller, my mentor.

I sat down with him and he said, "Tell me your dreams, young man. What are the possibilities for you?"

I said, "Well, sir, I would love to have inspirations like you do, write books someday, and share my inspirations with the world," and then I told him my dreams.

He said, "That's wonderful and marvelous. You know, there are many peaks and valleys, and you must focus on the peaks or the valleys can pull you down. Life is a peak-to-peak experience." And he went on to tell me a story about his television ministry.

It seems that his producers had come to him and said they needed at least $3 million by the end of the week or they'd have to discontinue his show. He was telling millions of people over the airwaves, "Have faith, and God will provide," but that week, God wasn't providing. He said he felt lost and in turmoil because $3 million was so far beyond his capacity at the time.

He said, "Young man, I didn't know what to do, so I went into prayer. I came to this office and I kneeled down, and I stayed here for three solid days, patiently waiting for a solution. During that time I thought, *I need 3 million people to donate $1, or 300,000 people to donate $10, or 3,000 people to donate $1,000. But how?*" Finally, after three days of prayer, an inspiring solution came to him: Don't just ask for something for nothing. Give them something for something.

Within minutes of receiving that message, Dr. Schuller came up with an inspirational quote and wrote it down. Then another and another seemed to flow out of him, and he wrote them all down. His inner voice told him to create something of value, a little gift or trinket with a quote on it that would inspire people, and then to offer it to them for donations—something for something. He went on the air that Sunday with a hastily put-together model, and much more than $3 million came in from people asking for those inspirational sayings.

The moment he decided to offer something of value, something he already had but didn't see until he searched for it, Robert Schuller received an influx of abundance. He invested in prayer and received an inspiration. He shared his inspiration and received an astonishing inpouring of wealth that empowered his ministry. Something for something all the way down the line.

He didn't ask for a handout, he gave people a hand *up,* and they did the same for him. When you begin to live your life in this way, the same miracles can happen for you. If you think you have nothing, why would the universe invest in you? Rather than focusing on lack and scarcity, acknowledge the great bounty of love, wisdom, and relationships you already possess, and start things moving. Physical, mental, or spiritual, fair exchange works.

The Secret of Charity

Many people believe that the act of giving is, in itself, noble and worthy. I don't deny that charity has a beautiful place in this world, but I would suggest a refinement in how you conduct it.

First, donate to causes that truly inspire you rather than just those where you feel the need to rescue. Second, don't let your donations to others get out of balance with your donations to yourself. And third, donate anonymously.

If you'd love to have increased wealth and results for yourself and others, invest in inspiration over desperation. Donate to individuals or causes you feel truly inspired by, ones that elicit tears of inspiration as guiding signs. Have you ever tried to rescue a friend who was financially desperate? The odds are that you said good-bye to your money *and* your friend because that was a foolish action, and a fool and his money are soon parted. Your friend wasn't managing the money wisely, then you gave more and it was managed the same way. Entropy is the tendency for things to break down, to go from an ordered to a disordered state, so every time you put money into a more disordered system than your own, entropy takes over and the system is further dissipated. The universe is trying to teach you to invest in higher order and inspiration, and when you don't, you receive a lesson.

Don't fall into the illusion that many impoverished people have, where their desire to give to their church or cause is so great that they wipe out their own assets. It's foolish to give all your money to a cause and nothing to yourself. It's wiser to divide it proportionately or equally between the two. If you do divide it in this way, the amount you'll accumulate in your half can later be donated (at or before your death), and it will be much greater than if you'd given it all away earlier. It makes sense to manage your money wisely and invest in yourself; otherwise, you'll live in poverty and have nothing lasting to pass on when you leave.

Those are the first two aspects of charity. But there's another and more subtle side to the issue.

Say someone comes to your door and says, "I'd like you to contribute to my cause." It could be education, disease eradication, saving forests or oceans or wildlife, a religion or a political party, or whatever, because the list is as endless as humankind's desire to make a difference in the world. If the cause inspires you and you make a donation, the recipient will be grateful, but guess what happens? Your name goes on a list and a year later they're back again. The second time around, you'll probably be less motivated to give, if only because it's been a year and the problem still hasn't been resolved. With each successive year, your desire to donate is likely to decrease. At the same time, their gratitude diminishes because it's become a habit, and their expectation of your donation commonly goes up. You eventually feel obligated, and they become disappointed or resentful if you refuse. You fall right down the scale from *loving* to give to *wanting* to give, to *having* to give. Is that a smart way to approach giving?

The wisest way to give a donation, contribute to a charity, or tithe is to do it anonymously. When those who represent a charitable cause ask for your loving contribution, simply say, "Thank you, but no thank you." Once they're gone, if you're truly inspired to give, become creative and find a way to give in a completely anonymous way. Of course, it's actually a form of fair exchange more than giving, for you're about to receive an equally profound gift back.

Think about the difference. In the first instance, the recipient thanks you, and you may both get caught up in the praise-and-blame cycle of feeling good and eventually feeling bad about the whole exchange. In the second version, a person or organization whose cause you truly care about receives an envelope with cash or some form of untraceable money to help them fulfill their dream. Who are they going to thank? The only thing they can do is turn their eyes upward and say, "Thank you, God. Thank you, universe." They're not being robbed of dignity and expecting you to take care of them; instead, they're grateful to the entire divine universe. Training people to give thanks in that way is of a higher value. It gives them more appreciation for, and trust in, the universe. They don't just thank a *part* of the universe (you), they thank the universe as a whole—a much greater thanks!

Anytime you make an anonymous donation, you're rewarded with a secret amount of charitable power. The vital key to maintaining this fair exchange and measure of power is to *never* tell another soul about it, not even your closest loved ones.

Have you ever had an inspiring secret that you kept quietly in your heart? The inner feeling generated by this type of secret is a powerful wealth builder; its power is equal to or greater than the amount of money you give. When you help someone become grateful to the universe, you're rewarded indirectly. But the instant you tell anyone about your secret, you disperse this magic quantum of energy and it becomes just another praise-and-blame, pride-and-shame game.

I invite you to try out this form of charity. It doesn't matter whether the amount you donate is $5 or $5 million; remember, the three keys are to donate to causes that truly inspire you, keep your giving in balance with your receiving, and donate anonymously and discreetly. The magic is in your motivation as well as in your silence. The difference between wise charity given anonymously and unwise desperation giving is vast. That's why it's unwise to give from a state of pity, guilt, or from an "Oh, those poor people" form of compassion. Desperation resue often perpetuates the very concern you're attempting to save. There's a far more enlightened way to achieve your charitable ends: By donating anonymously, you'll feel a certain timeless fulfillment inside. This feeling is a greater quantum of self-worth, a form of exchange that turns charity into a metaphysical investment, and the metaphysical return will be self-evident once you try it. Anytime you invest in inspiration rather than desperation, your inner self-wealth grows. Use your charity and your life wisely so that you continue to grow more grateful as long as you live.

Two Sides of the Fair-Exchange Equation

When you have difficulty receiving, you impede your giving. Likewise, when you have difficulty giving, you impede your receiving. Because the universe remains in perfect balance, these two sides of the fair-exchange equation are synchronous and balanced, even though they're not initially and outwardly apparent to most people. The universe conserves its creations and destructions, its giving out through white stars and taking in through black holes. You're no different. Anytime you imagine yourself giving something for nothing or getting something for nothing, you lower your perceived self-worth. It's your self-worth that determines your self-wealth or what you'll allow yourself to be, do, and have in life. Your heavenly self-worth is directly proportionate to how well you can equalize and maximize your giving and receiving.

The terms *giving* and *receiving* can be expanded into *giving service of value to others* and *receiving rewards of equal value to yourself.* In giving service, it's certainly wiser and more fulfilling to give the service you love and love the service you give. Likewise, in receiving rewards, it's wiser and more fulfilling to receive the reward you love and love the reward you receive.

It's wise to determine the form of fair compensation for any loving service given. If you provide a service to someone without predetermining a fair reward, you potentially diminish your self-worth and ultimately the self-worth of those you serve. Clearly defining what you would love in return for your service frees others from having to guess what their payment form can be. Not doing so lowers the value of the service you provide them because they feel uncertain, out of exchange, obligated, or undeserving. People tend to place more value on the things they pay for anyway. Payment doesn't necessarily have to be limited to currency, but payment does mean some designated form of exchange that fulfills an equal value in your life. It may be money, appreciation, relationship, prestige, or any other means of compensation, but it's vital to designate what you would love to receive for what you would love to give, to designate your inward value for your outward service.

Although these two sides of exchange are ultimately balanced, they're waiting for you to clearly determine their specific form. The moment you do, you become freed of past and future entanglements and uncertainties, and enter into a heavenly and grateful state of order and true presence. In this state of presence, you inspire others to do the same for themselves. By practicing fair exchange, you express fair and equitable blessings for all.

The following exercise will help you cement your understanding of the value of fair exchange and get you ready to look at the power of appreciation, the subject of the next chapter.

Exercise

Look back over your life and think of someone to whom you feel you owe a debt; someone who gave you money, time, support, or a gift; or a kindness that you don't feel you repaid adequately. When you identify that person, do either or both of the following things.

1. Ask yourself, "What did I do to deserve what I received from them?" In your journal, write down all the ways you earned the gift. Keep writing until you feel that you're back in equal exchange. When you discover enough ways, or hit the big one, you'll have an unmistakable sensation of release. It will be like an unconscious tension relaxing, or an invisible wall coming down and your whole perception of that person changing.

2. If you can't see how you earned what they gave you, ask yourself, "What could I do for them or give to them that would equal what they gave to me?" Then do it. This can really open your heart to anyone you've been keeping on the outside, either consciously or unconsciously.

Keep going with every single unbalanced relationship you can remember throughout your entire life, and follow the same steps with them all. Find out either what you've already done to deserve what you received (in which case the imbalance was only in your perception), or what you *could* do to deserve it, and balance it out in your consciousness. You may repay people for the gifts you've been given with money, a gift, a letter of true appreciation, or heartfelt words of acknowledgment. Do whatever feels appropriate, but awaken or return to fair exchange and watch the effects on your life unfold.

This exercise will bring into balance and back into the present any mental fragments that have been scattered throughout a lifetime of perceived imbalances. Eventually, you'll learn to do these steps spontaneously, *at the very moment of interaction,* bringing you a quantum leap in your power and potential. The truth is that every exchange is already balanced, whether you know it or not, but not until you see and feel it will you get your energy and freedom back.

Words of Wisdom and Power

- *I give and receive equally, for I maintain fair exchange.*

- *I give what they love, and I receive what I love.*

- *I give something for something—what they love for what I love.*

- *I know that something for nothing or nothing for something is an illusion.*

- *I receive what my work is truly worth.*

- *I invest in inspiration, not desperation.*

- *The world is in perfect order, so I serve and am served.*

Chapter Three
The Power of Appreciation

"Gratitude is heaven itself."
— William Blake

WHAT TO do with money will be covered in an upcoming chapter. For now, we're going to look at *why* you would be wise to appreciate and value money. Your future heaven or hell is partly dependent upon it.

Can your feelings of appreciation affect your degree of wealth? They certainly can. Grateful appreciation is a magically attractive force that can draw to you whatever you give thanks for. The converse is also true: Ungrateful nonappreciation generates an equally powerful repellent force. You have the power to create a financial heaven or hell for yourself because, like everything else in life, your finances respond to your feelings of gratitude or ingratitude.

One of the qualities of the *truly* wealthy is that they appreciate their wealth. Until you learn to value or appreciate wealth, it won't remain yours. If someone gave you a beautiful bronze statue and you just threw it in the back of your closet without a word of thanks, would they be likely to give you another? Of course not. They'd think, *You don't appreciate my art. I'd rather give it to someone who does.* When you don't appreciate your relationship partner, what happens? You eventually repel him or her. If you don't value and understand your clients, they stop coming.

Now personalize the universe for a moment and imagine it doing the same with you. If the universe gives you some giftlike opportunity and you don't appreciate it, eventually it says, "It's unwise to give this person a gift at present." The universe is teaching you to love and appreciate all aspects of your life, and it does so by giving when you appreciate and taking away when you don't. The quantity and quality of what you receive in life is proportionate to your degree of appreciation. Money and wealth are no different, and when you don't love and appreciate them, they go to the people who do.

Wealth grows or appreciates in value where and when it's appreciated, and knowledge is a vital key to that growth. If you go to an art gallery, your ability to appreciate the pictures is partly determined by how much you know about painting. The greater your knowledge of oils, varnish, light, perspective, brushstrokes, art history, and all the other details of painting, the deeper your appreciation. If you appreciate your loved ones, you not only give them attention, you also honor them by knowing their values and what's important to them.

In fact, appreciation *is* life, and increased knowledge brings increased appreciation and greater life. *The more you investigate, study, and understand the laws that govern wealth, the more you'll be able to appreciate and master managing money, and the more it will flow to you and grow for you.*

Many people say, "I'd love to be wealthy and prosperous, but I don't want to have to study all that stuff. It gives me a headache to even think about it." Yes, it's hard for these people to apply themselves to something they know nothing about, but why would wealth come into their hands when they haven't taken the time to value it? Learning the laws of wealth is one of the signs that you appreciate it. You're saying that it's worthy of your time, attention, and life, and whatever you appreciate, grows. The greater your knowledge, the easier your task. You already have more knowledge of the laws of wealth than when you began, so let's continue to build with a few personal applications.

> *"For in truth great love is born of great knowledge of the thing loved."*
>
> — Leonardo da Vinci

Start Your Engines

So far we've dealt mostly with the philosophy and psychology of heavenly wealth, but now it's time to delve deeper into the practical, earthly side: money. One of the most vital bits of knowledge required for building wealth is a detailed list of your present financial status. The clearer your picture of the present, the faster you can begin to grow your financial future.

I once consulted with an extremely wealthy gentleman in New York who took me on a guided tour of his huge home. An entire wall of his library was taken up with nothing but shelves filled with file after file, in alphabetical order, of everything he owned. Every single one of his assets had a corresponding file on that wall—from his cars, homes, investments, and jewelry, to his $250,000 chandelier and his $500,000 imported Egyptian fireplace. The files were beautifully organized with the cost, place, and date of purchase and updated appraisals and photographs, and all the information was duplicated in a condensed form in his safe. That man had great wealth, and he knew exactly what and where it all was. Did he do this from obsession or greed? No, he devoted his valuable time because he knew the importance of this principle: *When a financial house is organized, it receives more money than when it's not.*

Those with great economic mastery know how much money they have, where it's invested, how much it's earning, and what all their assets and liabilities are. They know their true net worth and therefore end up with much more. Contrast that with the average person who has little wealth and doesn't know how much it's worth, where it is, what interest it's earning, or how much insurance it's covered by. If you don't believe me, you can prove it to yourself by asking a random selection of people what they're worth. If they'll tell you, you'll find a direct correlation between their wealth and their knowledge about it.

To increase your knowledge and your wealth, start organizing your financial house by making a list of everything you own: every investment, insurance policy, possession, and asset. Create files for everything of value. Those who plan, organize, and appreciate their assets do far greater financially than those who don't. If you've never figured out your net worth, this is your opportunity. If you're living in a financial fantasy world, how can you expect to get ahead? It's a real wake-up call to find out where you are, truly decide where you would love to go, and begin laying out a plan to arrive there. Those who embrace this reality check and challenge are more likely to achieve their dreams than those who won't. I promise that if you take the time to organize your wealth, you'll receive economic rewards, because once your mind knows exactly where you are, it can take you farther down the heavenly road to financial freedom. But motivation is crucial for commitment to anything, including finance, and what follows can be a real money motivator.

Future Shock

This next exercise is a reality check to wake you up and help you gain a new appreciation of money. The experience may be somewhat shocking, but unless you get grounded in reality about your finances, you're unlikely to ever develop wealth.

Take out a clean sheet of paper. At the top center, write down your present real annual cost of living. Just below this amount, put the cost of living you'd have if you were to live today the way you would love your lifestyle to be, your reasonable ideal. Now add the two figures together and divide the total by two to get your averaged cost of living (the average between your real and your ideal). For example, if your real cost of living is $40,000 and your ideal cost of living is $100,000, you'd add them together to get $140,000. Then you'd divide by two and get your averaged cost of living, or $70,000.

Present real cost of living:	$ 40,000
Reasonable ideal cost of living:	+ $100,000
Total:	= $140,000
	÷ 2
Averaged cost of living:	= $ 70,000

Like everybody, you have two sides to yourself: a part that builds you up greater than you presently are, and a balancing opposite part that puts you down and makes you feel less than you presently are. Right between the two is who you probably are, and that's what your averaged cost of living represents.

Now, below your original calculation, on the lefthand side of the page, write your age. Just below it, write your averaged cost of living. Then move a little to the right and add 15 years to your age. Just below that figure, write double the amount of your averaged cost of living. For example, if you are 40 years old with a $70,000 averaged cost of living, the next column will be 55 years old and $140,000. Repeat the process and double the amount every 15 years, up to age 100. At 70 years it will be $280,000, at age 85 it's $560,000, and at age 100 the amount is $1.12 million. Most people end up with a total cost of living somewhere between $250,000 and $2 million at age 100.

40	55	70	85	100
$70,000	$140,000	$280,000	$560,000	$1,120,000

I use 15-year increments because of the diluting phenomenon known as inflation, the relatively constant erosion of the value of a dollar over time due to the additional printing of money. A financial principle called the Law of 72 says that if you divide the rate of inflation into 72 years, the result will be the number of years it takes to double the annual cost of living. Since the rate of inflation has averaged 4.8 percent over the last 100 years, we divide 72 by 4.8 percent to get the doubling rate: 15. This tells us that every 15 years the cost of living will probably double. If it seems hard to believe, just remember how much a car cost 25 years ago, how much you once paid in rent, or how much a suit or dress once cost. Although there are brief periods where deflation occurs, inflation is a more common trend of economic life.

Coming back to our exercise, if you began with $70,000 a year at age 40, and doubled the figure every 15 years, you discovered that it will cost about $1.12 million a year to maintain your averaged cost of living by the age of 100. If your starting age is older than 40, it may take slightly less; if you're younger, it may be slightly more.

So where's all that money going to come from? Certainly not all from the government. You'll need other sources of income, but at age 100 you may not be able to work anymore. That leaves inheritance, savings and investments with simple or compound interest, or passive income sources. Maybe you'd better figure how much principal you'll need in order to generate $1.12 million a year in interest.

Over the long haul, the interest on savings and investments averages about 8 percent per year, or one-twelfth of the principal. To figure out how much it will take to produce your averaged cost of living, multiply that figure by 12. Using our example, we'd multiply $1.12 million (desired cost of living at age 100) by 12 and get $13.44 million. In other words, you'd need $13.44 million in principal to yield $1.12 million a year in interest. Of course, if you lived on the principal amount and not just the interest, eroding the principal gradually, the total amount required in savings would be less.

Right about now, you may be wondering whether it will truly take that amount just to live that same lifestyle. Consider the following information. In the 1960s, financial planners encouraged their clients to plan for 60 percent of the annual cost of living as the target to aim at upon retirement (not that I actually recommend retiring). In the 1970s, it was 70 percent. By the 1980s, the figure was 80 percent, and by the 1990s it was 90 percent. Now that we're in the

21st century, I believe it's wise to plan on needing 100 percent of your annual averaged cost of living after the age of so-called retirement. I'd rather be on the high side than the low side any day.

And that's only to *maintain* that lifestyle, but you probably wouldn't love to stay there, would you? If you're reading about making a hell of a profit, I'm guessing you don't want to stagnate. You probably have a natural desire to keep expanding and raising the standard and quality of your lifestyle.

That brings us to the next question: Are you on track to save almost $13.5 million? I can tell you that most people aren't.

The reality is that most people don't think. They don't anticipate, they don't plan ahead, they don't even imagine their future. They just assume that somehow things will be taken care of, and they're completely unprepared for inflation and costs to eat up their savings. Or they may think a little, but only about the near future. They live with the desire for immediate gratification and think only about what they want and need right now. For them, short-term thinking means becoming a slave to time and money. Without some kind of very rare financial miracle, these people increase their chances of becoming dependent on a form of welfare later in life.

Make sure you have more money left at the end of your life,
than life at the end of your money.

Some people say, "God is taking care of me and all will be well," but they often become dependent upon their loving children or friends, or become forced to substantially reduce their standards of living. They may be taken care of, but it may be at the bare minimum unless they take steps now to ensure the standard of living they feel they deserve. God helps those who help themselves.

When I visit my frail mother in her retirement home, I regularly hear the elderly say, "I'd rather die than be a burden to my children." I believe this kind of thinking gives older people an incentive to stop living. They count up how much money they have left and figure out how long it will last them, and it's amazing how often they die according to that schedule.

I doubt that anyone sits around thinking, *I can't wait until I'm older so I can live off my children.* We have an inherent integrity that wants to achieve a certain quality of life without relying on or burdening anyone else. But without a long-term plan or strategy in place, that's exactly what may happen.

My parents' goal was to save at least $1 million, and they did it. Sounds like a lot, doesn't it? The problem was that they'd bought a ranch they couldn't maintain when they got older due to their illnesses, and they had to sell it relatively undervalued during a real estate downturn. They moved into a retirement home that cost $70,000 a year. Then, because of their illnesses, they spent enormous sums on medication, *quadrupling* their monthly cost of living at a time of life when they couldn't work. Their $1 million began evaporating faster than they could believe.

The purpose of this exercise is to make you stop and ask, "Have I even considered this? Have I planned and prepared for my financial future?" So if you skipped over this exercise, I urge you to go back and do it. Write down what you live on and what you hope to live on, take the average between the two, project it into the future with a doubling rate every 15 years, see what that number demands at 8 percent interest, and then *wake up.* That single act could be the most important financial step you ever take, shocking enough to motivate you to start putting a value on your wealth. It may make you say, "Hey, I'd better start studying about money and wealth," or "I really am living in a fantasy world, imagining that my family or inheritance or God or the state lottery will take care of me."

I offer these pointers not to frighten you, but because I care. You can grab hold of this idea right now and transform your own financial future, or you can wait until that future arrives and try to deal with it then. That which you don't presently appreciate will eventually humble you and direct you to honor it, because every aspect of life is ultimately worthy of love and appreciation. That doesn't mean infatuation, sometimes taken to be greed, because those who are infatuated with money are run by it and will eventually resent it, while those who truly appreciate money get to run *it.*

The medium of money is simply an efficient means of expressing the universal principle of fair exchange. If you depreciate money, it walks away from you; the people who say they don't care about money and material things are often the ones who ask you to buy them a cup of coffee or help them pay their rent. Those who try to deny the value of wealth will be denied it in turn until they learn to appreciate it. But when you appreciate money, it walks right up and asks how it can give itself to you. Like a garden, like a life, wealth flourishes when it's appreciated.

The future and the power are yours if you choose to embrace them. By planning the fine details of your financial future, you can begin to live more fully in the heavenly present.

Whoever appreciates nothing, receives nothing.

Love That Cat

The principle of appreciation applies not only to subtleties like finance and consciousness, but also to dense material objects. Your consciousness is a field, an intangible force, and it powerfully influences the materials and circumstances around you. This "mind field" is linked to the infinite creative potential of the divine, and you can access it through the power of gratitude or appreciation.

Have you ever gone into an area of town that was run-down and seedy, where everywhere you looked things seemed to be decaying? Maybe you saw rusty burned-out cars, abandoned stores, potholed streets and broken sidewalks, and litter everywhere. Scientific theories held that those depressing conditions created a similar state in the minds of the people who lived there, but a few years ago a very interesting phenomenon was observed. Civic reformers went to a poor city neighborhood and completely restored it. They hauled out the garbage, fixed the roads and sidewalks, restored the streetlights, painted the houses, and created public parks and gardens with benches. It was an amazing transformation, and they expected to see the same effect on the people who lived there. To their astonishment, when they went back a year later for a follow-up survey, they found the neighborhood almost exactly the way it had been before the "rescue." How was this possible?

The reformers didn't permanently change the conditions of the people living there because they were working under an incomplete assumption: that *environment alone creates the state of consciousness.* They left out the other side of the equation: that *consciousness also creates the environment.* The expression "mind over matter" exists for a reason.

Environments break down faster when they're unappreciated, while areas where people appreciate and take care of their homes and businesses remain more stable. It's not just maintenance and upkeep that produces results, it's also the state of *mind.* That's why heaven is represented as a place of beauty and hell is depicted as a barren wasteland or fiery pit: because they describe states of mind with and without appreciation. If you depreciate a relationship, you're asking for it to break down. If you depreciate your car, it will fall apart on you. In both cases, you can feel like you're in hell.

I learned this lesson when I worked very hard early in my career to fulfill my once-held dream of owning a Jaguar. I scrimped and saved, searched everywhere for exactly the right car, and when I finally found it, I drove it proudly off the used-car lot in a state of deep infatuation and pride. But I wasn't really appreciating that car. It was a bit of an ego trip, and the lesson wasn't long in coming.

Because I had bought it from a used-car dealer, the car was in less than perfect condition. It was four years old and, unknown to me, had been badly damaged before I bought it. The seat had a fault, and after I'd driven less than a block, it let go and left me lying flat on my back, looking up at the ceiling of my expensive new car. I couldn't sit up or see anything, so I got out and pushed the car back to the dealers, where I found that the parts were under warranty but the labor would cost me $700. Needless to say, I was pretty upset.

On my way out, I passed a little 70-year-old lady sitting at the front desk, peering through her glasses at an old typewriter and occasionally pecking at the keys. She was the owner's grand-mother, and without even looking up, she said in her high, cracked old voice, "Make sure you're nice to the kitty." I walked out looking over my shoulder and thinking, *What the . . . ?*

I picked the car up a few days later, drove it home, and parked it in my garage. When I backed out the next morning, a huge cloud of black smoke came pouring out. I called a tow truck and took my unappreciated car back in. As I passed the old lady, again she said, "Make sure you pet the pussycat."

The next time I got the car back, it wasn't long before all the rubber lining fell off the doors and they wouldn't shut. This went on and on like a nightmare, and I ended up spending $9,000 to get that #@*$! car on the road. My initial infatuation became my resentment.

The last time I returned to the car dealer's, I came out grinding my teeth, and there that little old lady was again. By now I was expecting some crazy kitty, remark from her, and sure enough she said, "Make sure you're sweet to the kitty." I'd had about enough, so I walked over and blurted out, "Ma'am, what's all this kitty stuff? Every time I come in here you talk to me about cats. Are you missing your kitty, or are you going senile?" She just smiled at me and said, "No. I've been in the Jaguar business for many years, and I *know* what I'm saying."

"Well, what *are* you saying?"

"Let me tell you a secret, young man. Jaguars are sensitive little pussycats. If you aren't nice to them, they'll bite you and scratch your eyes out! You have to appreciate them if you want them to respond." That kind of stopped me, because I knew I'd been cursing the car and having all kinds of trouble, and maybe I was just desperate enough to listen. So I walked out to my car and said, "Hi there, kitty kitty kitty. We're going to be friends now, so if you need some milk or anything at all, just ask."

As I talked to my little jaguar *cat,* I began to be aware of and appreciate it as something more than just a lump of metal or a liability. Strangely enough, when I appreciated it, conditions changed dramatically. That little old lady was right, because your mind is a real force, whether you're dealing with cars, relationships, or wealth. That force can be integrative or disintegrative, it can build up or break down, and you decide which it will be by the simple act of being either appreciative or unappreciative. Appreciation can *save* and *make* you money, and it can transform circumstances in your life as if by magic. In this next story, it did all three.

The Hit Men

Like everything else, from the atomic to the astronomic, your inner divine soul has a meaningful purpose for being in this world. The more you can find the order and purpose in all things, the more you'll discover their underlying divinity and the greater your appreciation will become. Everything that happens to you is connected to your purpose. There are no mistakes. To know this from the depths of your being is to appreciate your life, and to realize that what may once have seemed most despised and hellish ultimately reveals itself as just another part of divine order. Every time you feel deep appreciation, doors open and your wealth takes a quantum leap in whatever area you focus on. Nothing is unworthy of love and appreciation, including your so-called enemies.

Years ago when I was still a practicing chiropractor, two men from a large securities firm came to see me on the recommendation of a colleague. They were financial brokers and asset-protection specialists, and they were having a major problem with someone in their company. When they saw the sign on my door, they said, "We're going to a *chiropractor* to solve our financial issues?" You could say they were somewhat skeptical.

As these high-powered financiers looked around my office with some amusement, I asked them, "So, what seems to be your concern? How can I help you?"

"Well, we're not exactly sure," one of them said. "What's your background?"

I said, "Gentlemen, my fee is $500 per hour. Do you want to hear about my background, or do you want to address your issues?"

"Uh, okay," they said. "We have a financial opportunity here that's worth a *lot* of money to us, and this nervous bean counter is blocking the deal. He's higher up in the organization and won't pass our investment- and asset-protection proposals."

I said, "Okay. Any other problems?" and they looked at each other wide-eyed, as if to say, *He thinks he's going to solve something this big just sitting at that desk?*

They asked, "What are we going to do, then?"

When I said, "We're going to love him," they almost fell out of their seats with laughter!

"And we're going to *pay* you to do that?" they asked.

"Yes, you are," I replied, and at that point I took them through a methodology I've developed called the Quantum Collapse Process. The basic process is set out in *The Breakthrough Experience*, but basically it's a scientific method that helps people break through their limitations and find love and appreciation for anything in their lives.

I went to a whiteboard, asked them what this bean counter had done, and began writing it all down. They had a long list of complaints: "He's an idiot. He interfered with our proposal. He's shallow-thinking. He's an asshole. He's petty, stupid, egotistical, a powermonger, non-risk taking," and they went through all his negative attributes. They told me they were so angry and the deal was so big that they had jokingly considered bringing in a hit man to "knock off" the guy.

I said, "All right, who sees *you* as an idiot?" and I spent several hours taking them through the whole list, helping them to see where they were perceived as idiots in the eyes of others, where they had blown money and interfered with deals, until we found every trait in both of them. I kept after them until they could own 100 percent of all the traits they had projected onto the man. Their cockiness transformed into deep humility, so I then asked, "Now, what are the benefits of this man?" With some prodding, they came up with about 40 admirable qualities.

They said, "Hmm. We never thought that fully about him. I guess we missed seeing the other side of this man."

I said, "I know, because you simply didn't look. Everything has two sides, but you don't see them unless you truly and fully look. Did you ever not look because you wanted to be right?

Whenever you fellows have the choice between being right and being love, choose love."

What I didn't know at the beginning of our conversation was that two years earlier this man had, in their eyes, "sabotaged" another deal. When they told me about that episode, I asked, "If he hadn't 'sabotaged' you, what would have been the drawback?"

"There wouldn't have been any drawback. We would have gotten our deal!"

"No, find the drawback," I insisted. "You never get a pain without a pleasure, nor a pleasure without a pain."

That's when they were fully humbled. One of them suddenly went quiet, and he looked at his partner and said, "We'd be in prison today." His friend paused and then said, "My God, you're right! We forgot some details with offshore trusts and asset-protection systems that the Internal Revenue Service would have jumped on, and this man was the one who actually caught them." They would have ended up in prison or in court with a huge lawsuit from clients charging them with tax evasion. At that moment, they looked at him differently.

Then I said, "Because he 'sabotaged' that deal, did you go back to the drawing board and birth this new idea?" They looked at each other and nodded. "And are all the potential pitfalls and kinks worked out now? Did you get the lawyers and the IRS involved to make sure it's all clear and legal?" Again, they nodded. "What's this worth to you now?"

"Possibly millions of dollars."

"Did you ever thank him for helping you build a strategy worth millions of dollars?" They shook their heads. "What do you think of this 'asshole' now? Is there anything standing in the way of loving him just as he is?" When they saw how much the man had served them, they could barely speak, and they both had tears in their eyes.

One finally pulled himself together and said, "We ought to give him a cut of the deal. He's earned the right to be a part of this." And the other said, "You're right. He deserves it."

In just a few hours of truth, they'd gone from jokingly wanting to murder the man to offering him a part of their potential fortune. Their hearts were open and their minds clear. They saw a bigger picture, they saw the divine order and how it made them greater, and they deeply appreciated the man they'd despised. Once their resentment was transformed into appreciation, he passed their deal through immediately, without their saying a word to him. We met on a Friday, the deal went through on Monday, and the man didn't even want a cut.

You have the magical ability to do the same at any time with anything you truly appreciate, and the greater the appreciation and love, the more profound the effect.

Whatever you think about and thank about, you bring about.

Divine Order

There are three levels of appreciation. The first level is the superficial appreciation you feel when someone positively supports your values. The second level is the appreciation you feel when someone both supports and challenges your values and you've come to realize that both forms of their feedback serve you and hone you into your more fruitful and balanced state of being. The third level is the appreciation you feel when someone simultaneously supports and challenges your values, and their positive and negative feedback becomes so fully integrated that you feel only blessed by the integrity of their love.

The third level occurs when you see neither positive nor negative, only the honest wholeness of their union. This blessing reveals a perfectly balanced divine order in your life, where you rise beyond the first and second levels of appreciation and open your heart in a profound moment of heavenly love. In this state, you have tremendous potential energy to influence and direct spirit and matter. The root of the word *divinity* means "to shine," and that's what you do when you're grateful for the balanced perfection of things just as they are. The radiant, magnetic force of love draws to you and helps you manifest whatever you love.

The power of appreciation applies not just to wealth, but also to life itself. Everything on this earth is worthy of your love and appreciation, everything is a part of the divine order, and that includes wealth in all its forms. The more you see this truth, the more you begin to realize that you're actually in heaven right now. Whatever you're appreciative of or grateful for makes up your heaven, and whatever you're ungrateful for makes up your hell. As long as you live in illusions and don't see the divine order outside, you'll be unable to live it from within—garbage in, garbage out. If you perceive chaos, you'll act chaotically and things will break down, but when you perceive order, you give order to the things around you and they grow.

Wisdom means looking at your life and realizing that every single person and event was perfectly designed to help you on your life path. You've seen that spirit and matter are just different frequencies of the same thing—light. Spirit is hidden within formless love and wisdom in the higher frequencies, and concealed as materialized form in the lower frequencies, but it's all light. Anything you see with love turns into opportunity and light, and light is the fuel that lets you take off. Anything you fail to see with appreciation and love is your illusion, and it becomes the baggage that weighs you down and holds you back financially. Appreciation raises your frequency and ingratitude lowers it, so appreciation literally lifts your spirit and brings you in communion with God and heaven without ever leaving this world. Magnificence in, magnificence out. When you can see it, you will live it.

When you see and appreciate the divine perfection that surrounds you, you give off a radiant light and bring harmony to yourself. You also share that light with all those around you who are capable of receiving it, and you spontaneously begin to lead. Leadership and self-mastery demand a willingness to acknowledge and give thanks to a higher intelligent order. Those who can do so are connected to something much greater than just their physical forms: They are imbued with the certainty and confidence to lead others who have not yet reached that depth of awareness.

People who say, "I can't wait until my life gets better," or "Life was better back then," are living in a temporal myth of powerlessness. They constantly disempower themselves by thinking that life is not magnificent *now,* but truth and power are present when you acknowledge that life *is* magnificent now. If you train yourself to live only in the past and future, and don't appreciate the now, then tomorrow and next week and next year you'll still be living in the past and future, and you may never embrace life in the present. Anything you don't love you'll try to change into what you think would be "better," but your idea of "better" may be an illusion. The term *better* assumes that it's not magnificent the way it is, but the way it is may be perfect after all. Love and appreciate today as it is and you're granted the power to make it what you would love it to be. Appreciation and love make true life. Without them, you're just living in quiet desperation instead of having a life of abundance and inspiration.

"You will find as you look back upon your life that the moments that stand out, the moments when you have really lived, are the moments when you have done things in the spirit of love."

— Henry Drummond

The great mystic Meister Eckehart said, "If I only had one prayer, it would be 'Thank you.'" Set aside time daily for thankful prayer and meditation to help you see and remember that all is done in accordance with a higher universal design. The most powerful prayer is one of gratitude for what is, as it is, not how you think it should be. The few who are grateful for what happens in their life and ask for inner divine guidance to direct them become the masters. Amazing things await you there, and wisdom and wealth flow from that source, so take the time every day for prayer, to talk to the universe and thank it for its blessings. Communicate with your inner spiritual nature and it will guide you, for it has great wisdom. Do it every day, trust it, and learn from it. Train yourself to say, "Thank you, divine universe, for my life just the way it is. Thank you right now, and in the past, and in the future. Thank you."

I am richly thankful for my life.

Exercise 1

Appreciation raises the frequency of your consciousness, and ingratitude lowers it. Whenever you fail to appreciate what you give and receive, you lower your potential energy and block the channels through which your heavenly wealth can flow.

Every time you pay a bill or write a check in a state of resentment or ingratitude, that's the message you send into the world. From now on, send a different message. Whenever you receive a bill or an invoice, give thanks that somebody appreciated you *so much* that they lent you money or gave you a product, service, or idea in advance. They had the confidence and trust in you to invest in you, and you're now writing a check of appreciation back to them. Remember the beauty of the saying "Payment is due when service is rendered."

Instead of begrudging the expense, remember how what you're paying for has served you, and pay that bill in a state of appreciation and gratitude. Give thanks for what you've already received, give thanks for being able to pay for it, and watch how it transforms your relationship with wealth. Rather than a sense of lack or loss, this creates a feeling of enrichment and abundance. When you feel different about sending wealth into the world, the world will feel different about sending wealth back to you. Transactions cease to be about gain and loss and become a flow. This is financial metaphysics, and it works.

Exercise 2

Go back to the beginning of this chapter and reread the section entitled "Start Your Engines." Follow the instructions for creating your own index of files, laying out in clear detail everything you own and everything you owe. List all of your assets and liabilities, and put your financial house in order. You'll find assets you didn't even know about, and you may find liabilities you were unaware of, but you'll know where you stand.

If you're really committed to building wealth, you'll take the time to do this exercise; if you're not, you won't. This is a test of wealth's value to you and your commitment to it. Knowledge really is power, and doing this exercise will give you definitive information about your financial status. This is the beginning of your Library of Wealth.

Words of Wisdom and Power

- *I am flowing with money.*

- *I have more money at the end of the month . . .
  than month at the end of my money.*

- *My knowledge of wealth building appreciates daily.*

- *I have a highly appreciating financial foundation.*

- *I plant flowers in my wealth garden and water them
  with appreciation.*

- *Whatever I think about and thank about, I bring about.*

- *I love and appreciate my heavenly wealth.*

Chapter Four

From Self-Worth
to Net Worth

*"What a man thinks of himself, that it is which determines,
or rather indicates, his fate."*

— Henry David Thoreau

IN THIS world, you ultimately receive exactly what you feel you deserve, no more and no less, and this chapter is about how to raise your "deserving" level.

When I was just 17 years old, I met a powerful 93-year-old man who changed my life. He did it by drawing out of me a profound and inspiring vision of my destiny that elevated my true worth and transformed my beliefs about what was possible for me. He taught me that when you can *see* it, you can *be* it. That extraordinary man gave me the affirmation "I am a genius and I apply my wisdom" and told me to say it every day for the rest of my life. Even though I was just a near-illiterate young surfer at the time, I trusted him and followed his guidance diligently. I've never missed a day of saying that affirmation in over 31 years, and I know it's one of the major reasons why I am where I am and who I am now.

What you believe and what you say to yourself has a tremendous impact on what happens to you and what kind of life you'll lead. You are the creator of your own destiny. You write the script of your life with every thought. The more respect and love you have for yourself, the greater and more financially rewarded your life will be.

Understand that being a genius doesn't mean having a high IQ or even a college degree. Those are just secondary attributes, and they don't guarantee fulfillment or wisdom. It took many years of experience before I finally understood what my affirmation meant: *To be a genius means listening to the voice of your soul, your inner being, and following its enlightened guidance.* That's all it takes, because that voice *knows* you, and one of its messages is that you are worthy of greatness. If you don't feel worthy of wealth, you'll find wealth hard to manifest and even harder to keep. But when you know you're truly worthy and you deserve to be, do, and have the greatest gifts the world has to offer, nothing can stop you. Life is a mind game, and self-worth is the key to the most powerful mind and inspired life. Who you think you are determines what you'll be and what you'll receive.

When you enter a new country, you must stop at the border and declare your goods. When you emerge in this body, it's equally vital to declare what you would love to make out of life. The more you declare and embrace, the more you'll receive. The universe is waiting for you to put a value on yourself, and you won't get any more or any less than what you declare. If you don't acknowledge the value of your unique expression of life, whatever form it takes, the world will keep devaluing it until you do. That's a blessing! It's a foolproof mechanism to teach you to put a value on yourself, and the universe will keep denying you your dreams and kicking you in the butt until you do. *You* set the standard, and the more you raise that value, the more you receive it.

Until you value yourself, don't expect others to. Those who put a value on themselves end up wealthy, and those who don't end up poor. It's a simple equation and purely a self-worth issue, so if you don't learn to value yourself, don't expect to have wealth. As you believe, so shall you receive.

I Am a Genius?

I gave a talk on self-worth and inborn genius about 15 years ago, and a lady came up to me afterward and said, "Dr. Demartini, I loved your speech. I'm a meeting planner, and I could arrange a series of speaking engagements for you if you're interested."

Of course I said, "Great, let's do it."

Two weeks later she called me to say, "I've got a real estate convention that wants you to inspire them to be more success-ful," and she gave me the time and place. I met her at the con-vention hall about 30 minutes before I was due to speak, and she said to me, "There's one thing I want to make sure of before you begin. *Please* don't get up there and repeat that 'I am a genius' thing you say."

"Oh, why not?"

"Because they'll think you're on an ego trip. Just promise me you won't say it. I have big plans for our business, and that would really mess things up."

I smiled at her and said, "I'll do what will inspire them, don't worry about that."

When I got up on the platform, the first thing I did was have everybody in the room say in unison, "I am a genius and I apply my wisdom." I could see her off in the corner of the room with her face in her hands, slowly shaking her head from side to side as if to say, *Oh my God, he's really blown it now.* I happened to be on fire that day and got a standing ovation, which just means that half the people were moved and the other half were afraid of being rejected by the half who stood up. (Remember, it's wise to nei-ther be elated by praise nor crushed by rejection, because praise and blame are simply illusions on the path to mastery. Just stay steady by knowing who you are, and don't let the outer voices overwhelm your wise inner voice.)

Afterward she said, "Well, you pulled it off. We squeaked through, but we have to make sure we don't do it again."

I said to her, "I prefer not to work with such constraints on the truth." The truth is that every conscious person has deep within him or her a wise genius.

The main reason she had difficulty with my affirmation was because she wasn't willing to acknowledge her own genius. The group was fine—they loved it because people inherently know the truth of their greatness, and we all have a part that loves to be reminded of it from time to time. You're a genius if you choose to acknowledge and act on it, and the world will treat you exactly the way you treat yourself. That lady was not yet ready to acknowledge her own genius and immortal nature, so she was limiting her influence and ability to reach the people she would have loved to associate with.

She's not alone in this illusion, as I found when author and publisher Louise Hay and I joined forces in one of her seminars years ago on the healing connection between mind and body. One of her exercises called for people to stand in front of a mirror, look directly into their own eyes, and say, "I love you. You're a beautiful and worthy person." It was astonishing to see how many people just couldn't do it. They blushed and stammered or even cried, but they couldn't tell themselves that they were worthy of love.

If you don't believe that you're worthy of giving yourself love, you won't believe you're worthy of giving yourself wealth. Strange as it may seem, a key to having great wealth is having great love and appreciation for yourself. Think about this: If your inner creative force loved you enough to give you life, who the hell are you to say you're not as worthy of wealth as anyone else?

"Knowing others is wisdom. Knowing yourself is enlightenment."

— Lao-tzu

Take Your Privates Public

Like every person on this earth, you have each of the many human qualities in your own unique form. Anytime you imagine that you're superior to someone else—that you're better looking, smarter, more spiritually awakened, have more money or success, have more connections and friends, or do a greater job of raising your children—you enter into an illusion. You're focusing on just that one aspect and ignoring the areas of life where you have exactly the opposite qualities in another form. There is balance here, too. The word *persona* comes from the Greeks and means "mask," and every time you minimize another and exaggerate yourself, you create a self-righteous persona that is nothing but a mask on your true nature. Likewise, anytime you think someone else is greater than you in any of those areas, you create a "self-wrongeous" persona, which is also a mask. Both masks limit your creative potential and genius. Both the self-righteous and self-wrongeous personas are distortions, and the more extreme the distortion, the greater the block to wealth.

Have you ever pretended you had something you didn't, or pretended not to have something you did? When you play either game, nature will force you to play the other side, to get you back to the truth. I love having fun with doctors at big conventions by asking them at the start, "So how's your practice doing?"

They often say, "Oh, it's great! Lately we've really been booming."

That's the typical Thursday-night story. On Friday, their practice is a little bigger, Saturday it's even more, and by Sunday they're *incredibly* successful. So on Sunday I'll say, "That's fabulous, because you're just the person I'm looking for to buy this product or donate to this cause."

Immediately they say, "Well, you know, I was doing really well until *Friday.* An unexpected emergency came up, so we just don't have the money." They'll play the opposite role and go from self-righteous wealth to self-wrongeous poverty. Neither is true, and both games distract them from true wealth-building presence. You grow the fastest and deserve the most when you can be exactly who and where you are. Your true power lives in the balanced truth.

The deepest truth is that you're simply light resonating with a dense vibrational form. Every human being is a hologram of the light that makes up humankind. That means you have exactly the same potential as any highly accomplished person; you just aren't believing and acknowledging it. But the instant you have it in your mind, you start enacting it in your body. The acting profession is full of stories about people who suddenly appear on the scene and, in a matter of weeks, jump through all the hoops and achieve great acclaim without waiting the 20 years it usually takes. Why? They believed in themselves.

I recently consulted with a fashion model in New York who had bulimia. She was slim and absolutely gorgeous to my eyes, but when *she* looked in the mirror, all she saw was fat and ugliness. She had great outer beauty, but her inner illusions kept her from seeing it. She had not yet awakened to her own divine nature and felt inwardly hideous and unworthy. She felt guilty about being bulimic, so I helped her find 50 ways that it had helped her life until she was grateful for having experienced it. Then we balanced out a few other self-judgments she was carrying around, and in that moment she shifted. Instead of anxiously trying to be beautiful to cover up her imagined inner ugliness, she completely relaxed and her beauty just radiated out. At that moment, her anxiety about modeling dissipated, and the original dream for her career returned—to honor beauty, grace, and self-confidence for women around the world.

We unwisely spend so much time trying to conceal the parts of ourselves we feel ashamed of or lessened by, yet *everybody* has them. We're holograms of positive *and* negative qualities, particles of light equal to all other lights. You have every great human quality as well as every base one, in your own unique form, and they all serve. If you had to make a list of every single thing you never wanted anyone to know about your life and then present it on national television, you'd be horrified. But if the prize for the most despicable and repellent list was $100 million, you might immediately switch from trying to be the most admirable person and compete to be the most despised. Your values would probably shift according to the payoff.

The point is that you certainly have "stuff"—beliefs and illusions—that you probably wouldn't like to lay on the table. It's called your private life, and self-worth and fulfillment have a lot to do with your ability to take your privates public. In other words, when you can take the things you judge in yourself and appreciate them to the point where it wouldn't matter if people found out, you'll attain real self-love. When you love yourself, people's opinions won't *touch* you. When you don't love yourself, people are mysteriously drawn to attack you because you're doing the same to yourself first. The world is a mirror that shows how you feel about yourself, and with self-love there's little fear of such reflection.

> *I would rather have the whole world against*
> *me than my own soul.*

Free Will or Freeloaders

When I first started out in practice as a chiropractor, I was very idealistic and altruistic. I thought, *I just want to heal for the sake of healing. Money is crass and unimportant. I love this so much, I'd do it for nothing.* My immature belief system said that as a true healer I should work for free, and that's exactly what happened. My desire to *give* for nothing attracted a whole lot of people who desired *receiving* for nothing, and slowly I got further and further into debt and stress. It was amazing how powerfully I drew in people who were unable or unwilling to pay for my services, who thought I was supposed to give my service for nothing, and who then referred identical friends. They seemed to be saying, "Well, you're a healer. Aren't you supposed to help us whether we can afford it or not?"

Many people go from doctor to doctor with a litany of stories and excuses in order to get free services. They're smart enough to target new practitioners just out of professional school who haven't yet developed self-worth, and until they do, those patients just walk all over them. The minute the doctor says, "That's enough. These are my fees," they go on to a new doctor. Are they parasites? No, they're teachers! They teach doctors to raise their self-worth. Whenever I mention this in health-professional seminars, the doctors all start laughing because they've been through it them-selves. The same thing happens in every occupation until the financial neophytes wake up.

For me, this went on until I awoke to what I truly desired, which was to be a great healer and be financially viable. I'd been repressing the other side of myself, but those early clients helped me become honest.

After a while, I got a little wiser and thought I could raise my value by bringing a lot of celebrities and sports personalities into my clinic. I hoped these people could make me more worthy, but what I got was another lesson. After 18 months, I dropped most of them because I ended up with a lot of prima donnas who wanted something for nothing. They demanded special treatment, didn't show up for appointments, and rarely paid their bills. I was distracted, wasted a lot of time, and lowered my dollar value without attracting any more clients. Finally, I decided I'd rather build my business until I became as wealthy as they were, and then attract them as equals. When I did, they paid, and they referred others who also paid. People know and reflect your self-worth, high or low.

Trying to receive or give something for nothing is a surefire way to lower your net worth. You're actually saying, "I'm of less value than you. What you'll do with my dollar is more important than what I can do with it." Money is very obedient and goes where it's valued, so if you say that someone else's use is more valuable than yours, the money will go to them. You don't lose in this world. Instead of getting the money, you get valuable lessons until you finally stand up and say, "I'm worth more than this! My use of the money is equally as important as yours." If they really desired your service, they'd find the money; they'd find a way.

With the intention of helping people, you actually support their low self-worth, rob them of dignity, and keep them from embracing responsibility for their own dreams. When you stop rescuing them, they either wake up and get motivated or go plug their umbilical cord into the next person who's ready to learn that lesson. In either case, lessons are learned.

Rescuing is very seductive. So many people think, *If I do this for nothing, I'll somehow be rewarded,* and it's a myth. When you try to give something for free, you attract freeloaders. Unless you acknowledge your worth and place a fee on your services, you won't receive what you'd love. Use your free will to say, "Yes, I'm also in it for some money, or the feeling of accomplishment," or whatever, and love that part of yourself, or the universe won't give it to you. It's like trying to give a birthday present to a friend who won't tell you what she wants. She knows exactly what it is, just as you do in your life, but she's afraid to say it—so you give her something she doesn't want! The test is being able to declare to yourself and the world what you'd really love to receive in exchange for your service. Once you're clear and have no fear or guilt about your reward, it begins to appear.

The universe is doing everything it can to get you to put a fee or at least a value on yourself. Have you realized that? It's trying to get you to say, "This is how much I'm worth," because until you declare it, people in the world won't honor it. The moment you do, you can have it. The universe will teach you lesson after lesson until you finally declare what it is you'd love to do, what you'd love to receive for doing it, and whom you'd love to be in the process.

The universe is your friend, trying to teach you, and it's willing to do whatever it takes to make sure you learn. It will give you challenges and lessons in every area of your life to wake you up to the profound principle that you can have whatever you would truly love and truly feel you deserve. Why would the universe bother? Because you are loved, and self-love is the lesson.

Mind Over Matter

On an airplane to Dallas one day, I met a former winner of the $8 million Texas lottery. We started chatting, and he told me that the first thing he'd done after winning the jackpot was to go out and buy houses for his mother, sister, and cousin; buy himself a big car; and invest the rest. He now owns five companies and has turned that $8 million into $10 million. He said to me, "The strange thing about it is, I was absolutely certain I was going to win that money. I actually went out looking for homes for my family before the numbers were even drawn." His fiancée sitting next to him nodded her head because she'd been with him the whole time.

Interestingly, the great majority of lottery winners lose all the money within five years, and many of them end up with less than they had before they won. Why? Because they don't feel worthy of their wealth, and it leaves them. This man's certainty had brought him the money, and his self-worth helped him manage and grow it.

By the same token, you deserve what you receive. There are two kinds of fortunes: those that are inherited and those that are made. If you inherit wealth and don't feel you deserve it, it probably won't stay in your hands. I consulted with a lady who had inherited $5 million but didn't feel she'd earned it, and that money was flowing out of her account like water through a sieve.

I said to her, "You couldn't have attracted that money unless you somehow inwardly deserved it. I want you to write down 200 ways you earned that money."

She said, "Oooh, that's an interesting idea," and for the next two weeks she listed the ways she'd earned the money. She wrote down things like hard work, generosity, kindness, gratitude for life, caring for others, creating beauty, dreaming about and asking for wealth, and having a great purpose for it. I didn't let her stop until she had a tear in her eye and could say, "You know, this money is mine. I truly do deserve it." From that moment on, the outflow stopped, and her desire to wisely manage her money awakened. She felt she'd earned it and didn't want to squander it anymore.

If you inherit wealth, sit down and list exactly how you earned it. Otherwise, you'll wipe it out in the false, unconscious belief that you don't deserve it. If you deserve it, you can receive it. If you receive it, know that it's yours.

Heartfelt Life

Another crucial factor of growing your self-worth is loving what you do. Unless you feel you're making a meaningful contribution to the world, you're unlikely to allow yourself to receive great rewards for your time here. You have an inherent sense of fair exchange, so the best way to receive more is to serve more.

The owner of a New York–based company that designed packaging for children's toys once called me in because he felt he was losing contact with his business. It had grown beyond his ability to monitor it, and he was increasingly depressed because he felt it had gone off track and was no longer fulfilling his original inspiration. His dream had been to have an impact on young people and make a difference in their lives, but the company was so big he didn't feel he was personally involved or impacting anyone. The larger the company became, the more disheartened he felt.

When we met, I simply advised him to put his hands on every piece of film, artwork, and literature his company sent out into the world. I said, "Make sure everything that goes out that door is touched by what's in your heart. See those children in your mind's eye, and let them receive the love you feel for them. Don't let anything go out without your awareness being included."

With that one act, he suddenly felt connected again and his heart opened up. The instant he stopped unconsciously resisting growth and put his heart back in his business, it took off. The firm had been dealing with many small projects and companies, but shortly afterward his clients included major corporations such as 20th Century Fox, Disney, and Wurlitzer. Opening his heart simultaneously opened the door to increased wealth and greater fulfillment.

Love It or Lose It

Anything that doesn't fulfill its purpose will self-destruct, from a relationship to a company to a life. People who complain that the world is unfair or unjust because others are being given so much while they're getting so little are creating that situation themselves, and only they can change it. The world is fair; you receive what you give. If you're not receiving in abundance, it's because you're avoiding the things that those who receive so much are doing. The moment you begin to listen to your inner voice and follow through on its directions is the moment magic occurs. Find your unique expression in this world. Honor yourself and do what you love. Let your wise inner voice guide you.

A 68-year-old gentleman came to my Breakthrough Experience program sometime ago. He'd retired and was doing virtually "nothing," as he called it—just puttering around, playing a little golf, and watching time pass. During the seminar, he had a big awakening with many tears, because he saw himself and his wife gradually decaying right before his eyes. He saw his mind lose its clarity, his body start to go, and his faculties shut down over a five-year period. Because of this vision, he had a major catharsis and opened up his heart. He said, "I just realized that I've had such a full life, with so much knowledge and so many experiences, and if I don't organize and be thankful for it and *share* that with others . . . I'm not fulfilling my potential, and I feel like I'm just going to die."

He opened his eyes and saw so many things he could be doing to value his time. Instantly, he looked five years younger. He had a purpose to live for, and he couldn't wait to go out and fulfill it. Now, with one of his old friends, he's consulting, and teaching seminars to young businesspeople.

Your self-worth is directly proportionate to how well you maximize and equalize your giving and receiving, in accord with the Law of Equilibrium, while doing what you love. That's the secret of bringing heaven to Earth: living with a whole spirit. As you approach it, you'll find yourself accomplishing things that most people wouldn't even imagine.

> *"If you want one year of prosperity, grow seeds.*
> *If you want ten years of prosperity, grow trees.*
> *If you want one hundred years of prosperity, grow people."*
>
> — Chinese proverb

Guts and Glory

Self-worth builds both creativity and courage. If you have great self-worth, you'll never have to worry about having a job because people are spontaneously drawn to this quality and want to employ or work for those who have it. If you have low self-worth, you'll have more difficulty acquiring a job, and if you blame others or make excuses for the way your life is going, you'll further lower your already low self-worth. You have either results or excuses, and they're mutually exclusive. If you take responsibility for your life and ask quality questions about how to fulfill it, you become a magnet for opportunities. People and money are irresistibly drawn to energy, enthusiasm, and certainty.

When I first opened my chiropractic practice, I had an 870-square-foot office in a shopping center. Nine months later, I expanded to 2,100 square feet with three doctors working for me. I gave introductory lectures in my little reception room rather than a hotel because I wanted people there in the clinic, to sign them up for care right away. Then, overnight, the boot shop next door went out of business and nearly 3,000 square feet of space became available. The space would make the perfect lecture hall, and I wanted to move in right away.

I tried contacting the leasing company, but when I didn't get a response, I hired a locksmith to open the space. I recarpeted and repainted, built a podium and lectern, put in some special lighting and 60 chairs, and I was off. I'd spent $30,000 on premises I'd virtually broken into, but I was expanding my business.

That same shopping center held a ten-cinema movie complex. I noticed that its maximum pedestrian flows were between 7:00 and 7:30 P.M., so I started giving my weekly "Health Education and Awareness Lectures" (HEAL) at that time, placing big loudspeakers in the parking lot to maximize exposure. I also hired a video company to tape all my talks, because I knew that cameras and lights attracted more people. Asking themselves, "What's going on over *there?*" people would be drawn to my talks. At the end of each lecture, I'd show them through the office and they'd become patients. I soon had one of the largest clinics in the city, but I had only a part of the full lease.

One day while I was renovating and adding more treatment rooms, a leasing agent finally visited, looked around in disbelief, and said, "What the hell *is* all this? What's going *on* here?" But I just said, "Excuse me, the man with the plasterboard has to get through." The leasing agent stormed out, and I didn't hear any more about it for a while.

We'd finished the work and I'd been operating and growing rapidly for about three weeks, when one day I came out of a treatment room and stopped cold. There in the hallway stood a man who had such overwhelming certainty and command that I could just feel it was *his place,* and I knew immediately who he was. He was the founder of the property-management company that owned shopping centers and real estate developments all over the city, and he just *radiated* self-worth. As he stood there with his arms crossed and no expression on his face, just looking slowly from side to side, I felt a stab of fear.

He looked over at me and said, "So *you're* Dr. Demartini."

"Yes, sir," I replied.

"Philip Freeman, Freeman Management Company."

"Pleased to meet you, Mr. Freeman."

"Impressive place you have here," he said, and I just nodded. "You know, you remind me of me. Tell you what. You've got six months free rent."

Now, you need to understand that I hadn't been completely reckless in my actions. I knew that vacant premises are generally a detriment to shopping centers and that if I made it work, the management would be pleased. I also knew that the company took months to get things done, and if I'd applied to open a lecture hall they'd have turned me down flat, so I took the risk and made it happen fast.

I would have been glad to sign a lease and pay back rent, but Philip Freeman didn't even request it. We kept talking, and he asked me about my background, my vision, and my goals, and then he said, "Would you like to open up franchises in all my shopping centers?"

"No, thank you," I said. "I'll just keep the one clinic. I'm transitioning into public speaking and teaching later."

"Okay," he said, "but if you ever want to come and work for me, I'm offering you a $250,000 salary. I'm looking for people like you."

That was more than I was making at the time, and it definitely made me blink for a second. Then I remembered that my vision was vastly bigger than that, and I didn't want to work for someone else and be confined or obligated there; I wanted open space for my consciousness to expand into my dreams. I thanked him for the opportunity, though, because it gave me greater certainty about my value in the marketplace.

Six months later, I received a powerful vision to move into a beautiful tower building. I sold my practice to the doctors working for me, closed the new section because it was too big for them to handle, and went to visit Freeman Management Company headquarters.

I said, "Philip, you're not going to believe this. I'm shutting the place down because I had a vision to move to a high-rise office building."

He laughed for a moment and then said, "You've got *guts,* my man! Okay, fine, no problem. You're out of the deal," and he ripped up our contract. Although I didn't pay directly for that rental space, and made a great profit on my outlay, the management company had received the benefit and economic return of my practice drawing business to their center. Philip was wise enough to see all the benefits he'd received. He was a real entrepreneur.

High self-worth is rewarded handsomely, and I was blessed with the rewards for the risks my certainty allowed me to take. Some people think they want life to be easy, but that's the definition of a small life. There's great power in challenging yourself. It takes you beyond who you think you are and reveals who you can be. When you're willing to do the things that other people aren't, and when you trust and honor yourself that much, the world honors you right back.

"The law of nature is, do the thing and you shall have the power:
but they who do not the thing have not the power."

— Ralph Waldo Emerson

You Are Divine Perfection

Deep within you is your tremendous inner being or soul. You serve yourself and the world most by acknowledging its magnificence, not by pretending to be insignificant or unworthy. No one wakes up in the morning and says, "God, I wish I could think small! I wish I could *have* less and *do* less and *be* less in my life!" Within everyone is an irresistible urge to grow and expand. You're destined for greatness. It's inevitable.

Acknowledge your inevitable destiny and it will unfold before your eyes. Just by being alive, you're already a winner. Out of 20 million sperm in that first race for life, you were the champion! You're already an expression of divine achievement—life itself —so acknowledge and live it to the fullest. Instead of dissipating your energy and time on illusions of unworthiness and imperfection, acknowledge that you're worthy of the magnificence life has to offer.

The heart is more powerful than the intellect when it comes to perceiving divine perfection, so listen to your heart's self-love rather than your head's self-judgment. I'm amazed by the number of people I meet every week who believe that they'll one day get to perfection, instead of acknowledging the perfection they are right now. They say, "Well, I'm not perfect, I'm only human. What do you expect?" They've bought into the illusion that perfection is unattainable. They haven't been taught to recognize the perfection that already *is*.

Maybe now is the perfect time to awaken to your divine perfection. Rather than judging and depreciating yourself, it's wiser to ask, "Where is God not? Where is divine perfection not?" Perfection is everywhere and in everything, including you, so no matter what you've done or not done, you're worthy of love, for you're a part of the magnificence. As Einstein stated, "If this being [God] is omnipotent, then every occurrence, including every human action, every human thought, and every human feeling and aspiration is also His work." And as Shantanand Saraswati stated, "If God is omnipresent and omniscient, then whose ignorance is it? You are in truth omnipresent and omniscient, and ignorance is only 'forgetfulness.' Ignorance belongs to the person who is asking the question."

No matter what, you're a part of divine perfection. You were created in love, and you deserve a part of all this world has to offer. When you awaken to that understanding, you have access to limitless creative energy that is unfathomable to average minds but attainable by the human psyche in a state of grace. You deserve to have your heart's desire, including fabulous wealth, and the moment you truly feel worthy, it appears as if by magic in your life. It *is* magic, and you're the magician who makes it happen. If God is love, love is divine. If you want the divine power to live your dreams, love yourself. Everything else will follow.

"Wherever you turn is God's face."

— Mohammed

Exercise 1

If you under- or overvalue yourself and obscure your true worth, you won't operate in a state of fair exchange. Instead, clear consciousness becomes clouded with uncertainties. People often say to me, "I don't know what I'm really worth," but in truth everyone inwardly knows. Mastery arises when you awaken to your true inner worth, and this exercise will help you find out exactly what that is.

You can either do this alone in front of a mirror, or work with a friend. Ask yourself, or have your friend ask you, "For your time, how much are you worth?"

Start with a ridiculously low figure: "Are you worth $5 an hour?"

If the answer is, "No, I'm worth a lot more than that," then go to a ridiculously high figure: "Are you worth $5,000 an hour?"

If you answer, "Uh, no, not yet," work your way in, alternately and incrementally raising the low figure and lowering the high one, until you find out exactly what you believe your time is worth. Alternatively, you can just keep raising the low figure until you find the financial level you resonate with. When you reach it, you'll know.

A young woman in the corporate world came to me and said, "I want to position myself at the top of the market, but I don't know what the fees are up there. How do I decide how much to charge for a one-day corporate training that isn't too much or too little?"

I said, "I can give you the exact price, but you have to answer some questions for me. Is it a dollar?"

"Of course not."

"Is it $100?"

"No way."

"Is it $500?"

"You mean I just have to decide?"

"No, just watch what happens. Is it $1,000?"

"No."

"Is it $2,000?"

"Nope."

"Is it $4,000?"

"No."

"Is it $5,000?"

"Um, no."

"Is it $6,000?"

"Too high."

"Is it $5,500?"

"Yes. Actually, $5,600 feels exactly right. Thanks very much."

She knew, and you know, too. Set your price according to the true worth that your heart already knows. If you go above that value, you'll feel you won't deserve it. If you go below it, you'll feel you deserve more.

The time you're charging for is your *life,* so the real question is, how much do you feel your life is worth? When you find that value, the one that your heart resonates with, stick to it and watch it grow as you do.

Exercise 2

Don't underestimate the power of your mind to create wealth. If you focus on it, it can happen.

Years ago, a man by the name of Charles Fillmore wrote a book called *Prosperity.* In it, he included a copy of a blank check and instructed his readers to make the check out for the amount and date they desired it to manifest in their lives. He also recommended that they put it in their Bibles. I figured there was nothing to lose, and a big potential reward to gain, so I tried it. I filled that check out for $1 million, payable to myself in two years—but it didn't happen. It took four! I have a client involved in the movie industry, and she said that Jim Carrey wrote himself a $10 million check that he carried around for years. His first big film paid him $10 million.

This is a real phenomenon. Write out a check payable to yourself for the amount you would love to have and the date you would love to have it, and put it in your wallet or a place that has meaning for you. Be sure the amount resonates with your true value. Just seeing and thinking about your name in association with that money is the first step to making it appear in the world. If you can see it, you can be it.

Words of Wisdom and Power

- *I am a financial genius, and I apply my moneymaking wisdom.*

- *Praise and blame are illusions on the path to financial mastery.*

- *I do what I love and I love what I do.*

- *I am worthy, for I am part of the divine perfection.*

- *When I see it, I will be it.*

Chapter Five

The Spiritual Laws of Saving

"Piggy banks become biggy banks."

— John Demartini

WE'VE LOOKED at how to attract wealth from the inside out, from a deep sense of personal worthiness, so now let's explore the other side of the equation: how to create a fortune from the outside in. What follows is a simple step-by-step program for building wealth, and if you commit to it, your finances will grow beyond what you may presently believe possible. Of course, it will require that you value wealth and have some discipline, but in life, the pain of regret, of what might have been, far outweighs the pain of discipline.

When I ask people in my seminars all around the world, "How many here have been working and earning money for years?" almost every hand goes up. My next question is, "And how many of you have saved very little or nothing of all the money you've made?" Again, most hands go up.

Americans, as wealthy as their nation seems, typically save only 1 to 3 percent of their incomes, and the rest of the world is not dissimilar. About 93 percent of the U.S. population depends on Social Security upon retirement, and the average check is about $1,200 a month. Roughly 69 percent of the people who end up surviving on Social Security also depend on their children to supplement that income with cash, accommodations, or food. That means that almost 70 percent could not make it without assistance. They may have made a million dollars or more in their lives, but what do they have to show for it?

In the late 1990s, a national newspaper reported that the average American was worth around $320,000 at retirement, $170,000 of which was invested in a house they couldn't sell because it wouldn't yield enough to pay for a retirement home. Their $150,000 in savings returns about $1,200 a month in interest, and added to their Social Security check, that gives them $2,400 a month. That's what they're surviving on, and when I ask my audiences how many people can't wait to have that sort of lifestyle, hands do not go up. The truth is that most people aren't on track with their savings to provide a decent lifestyle. They're living in a fantasy world and hoping that somehow everything will just take care of itself. If you continue at the rate you've been saving, are you on track for financial independence? Probably not! So let's look at how to turn your financial odds around, starting right now.

As you learned earlier, bringing order to your financial house helps you build wealth. In fact, the order itself is partly what draws money to you. Without order, finances break down. Order requires conscious intention and effort. Would you agree that it takes no effort to stay in bed, let your hair and nails and teeth go, and grow dirty? It takes effort to get up in the morning, put yourself together, and tackle the daily challenges of the world. By the same token, it takes no effort to be poor, but it takes planned organization and inspired effort to grow your money and become financially independent.

If you pay no attention to your finances, financial chaos can run your life. But if you take the time to master money, eventually it will work for you. Either you're working for money and potentially falling behind, or money works for you and grows ever faster. That's the big division between the "have nots" and the "haves"—one group spends their entire life working for money, and the other has learned how to make money work for them. Unless you're the master of money, you can become its slave, and it's an excellent servant but a harsh master. So what's the secret?

Save Yourself

One of the unrecognized contributions that computers make to our world is the suggestion that comes up on your screen every time you try to shut down: SAVE! Have you ever forgotten to save your hard work on your computer and it just disappeared? Well, the same thing can happen with your finances. If you don't create the habit of putting aside a portion of the money you earn, at the end of your life you could have little or nothing to show for your 50 years of toil. Without substantial savings, you could be in the 93 percent of people who end up dependent on some form of assistance. So, if saving is such a powerful source of wealth, why doesn't everyone do it? Perhaps it's because they believe they're partially controlled by the tyranny of their work and bills.

To overcome this believed tyranny, you must save. Accumulated money acts like a magnet: The more you have, the more you can attract. But if you're on a fixed income and bills eat up virtually all of your money, how can you attract more? Some people try to make their initial "money magnet" by taking a second or even a third job, but they still don't seem to achieve real wealth. They often cancel their money out by living beyond their means without saving, or by developing the tension and exhaustion that comes from uninspired overwork—working themselves to death when they really want an increased life. It's a dilemma that can break backs and hearts if left unsolved. The answer isn't to simply work harder, although productive work has a value, but to work *smarter.*

To work smarter and save, you must overcome any money illusions you may have. One common illusion is that money is limited. Since the universe is literally infinite, with inexhaustible, transformable resources, your financial possibilities are also unlimited. Your immortal self or soul knows this, but your mortal self thinks in terms of limitations and finites.

Your mortal self says, "Look, I only have a certain income, and all these bills have to come out of it. If I try to save money, I won't have enough to pay the bills." It's an either-or belief system, and *it's simply not true.* Your immortal self has more courage, discipline, and wisdom than this. It knows a great and powerful metaphysical secret: If you pay yourself first and save, you'll attract more money. No matter how much you make per month, whether it be $1,000, $10,000, or $100,000, take a portion off the top and put it into savings. When you save *first,* you magically attract more money to pay the bills.

I've introduced this principle to many people, and they later respond, "I tried your savings program and it was so weird! Even though I couldn't really afford it, I saved first and somehow money appeared from nowhere to cover my bills by the end of the month. What's going on here?"

Some people understand this principle more quickly, while others take longer, often because their rational minds insist that it just doesn't make sense. Eventually, everyone who perseveres with this principle comes to believe it. Why does it work? Well, maybe the world acts as a mirror, reflecting people's self-image. Or maybe it has an intention—that of growing consciousness and self-worth—and it rewards people financially who align with and help to fulfill such an intention. Maybe it blesses people with spiritual and material wealth by teaching them to pay themselves first. Or maybe it just rewards people for investing in their heart's inspirations and acting upon their priorities.

Priorities are important. Spending money wisely means spending it according to priority, and that priority is based upon whatever you feel is truly most important at the time or whatever will penalize you most if you don't pay for it. If you have a credit-card bill that charges you 18 percent and a doctor's bill that charges you nothing, which one will you pay first? The one that carries the penalty, of course. Whoever screams the loudest gets paid first. The more powerful the institution, the bigger the penalties they bring to bear to make sure they get paid, so you pay them to avoid the penalties. But of all the things you pay, ultimately your *self* carries the highest penalty if left unpaid.

Unless you reward yourself for the service you provide to the world, you'll eventually diminish yourself and your business. It's a sign that you haven't yet learned to love and honor yourself and your dreams. Therefore, the highest priority payment you can make is to yourself. People who are impoverished wait to pay themselves last. They pay all their bills first and themselves afterward. The wealthy automatically take the cream off the top—they pay themselves first and let everything else follow in turn, according to priority. They're saying, "I'm worth more than all those other things," instead of, "Everything else is worth more than I am."

The world reflects you, and until you're willing to invest in you, don't expect others to. But to the degree that you honor and invest in yourself, the world will follow at the same percentage. If you invest only one percent of all you earn in yourself, that's how much the world will invest. If you invest 10 percent, it will be matched. Whatever you save, the world will magically match for you. The world says, "Hey, you're acting as if you're really worth something instead of just talking about it," and then honors you in return.

People who say they're worth something but pay themselves last demonstrate that they really don't believe what they're saying—their actions contradict their words and nothing happens. *If you don't pay yourself first, why would anybody else?* You attract people into your life who pay you in direct proportion to how *you* pay you. If you wait and pay yourself last, then those you attract into your business and your life will put you at the bottom of the barrel and only pay you if and when they have extra money. The minute you start paying yourself first, the rate and amount that others pay you will go up, and money will begin to appear from sources you haven't even thought of yet. It's absolutely amazing!

Most people will never realize the tremendous power of this secret because it's too simple to believe and seems too hard to begin, and they're ruled by their fear of not having enough. That's a poverty-complex mentality based on lack and limitation, and it inevitably creates more impoverishment. If you're ready to step out beyond that fear, let's look at how to go about it.

The Immortality Account

What's an immortality account? It's the account you set up to grow the savings you give yourself first, before any other expenditure. Why immortality? Because you're made up of two components: a mortal body and an immortal soul. Your mortal body is ruled by its emotions, by fear and doubt, and it lives within a limited time frame. It tells you what you must do to survive, which means just getting by. Your inspired soul isn't concerned with survival because it's immortal and can't die, and it calls you to do what you love.

The purpose of the immortality account is to free you up to live your life from your soul, to eventually make more money from interest and investments than you can make by mortally working. When you reach that point, your life will be utterly transformed. That's a day of certainty—when you no longer work because you feel you have to, and you can choose to do only what you love. When you wake up every morning with that freedom, you'll not only be wealthy, you'll feel like you're experiencing a little bit of heaven right here on Earth.

The power of your immortality account hinges on your ability to make a valued decision and stick by it. Once the money is put into the account, *it's no longer yours to spend,* at least immediately. From that moment, it belongs to your immortal soul and has been dedicated to your future heavenly wealth. It's not to be touched or used for any mortal purposes—not for paying bills or taking vacations or meeting emergencies. The only time you do anything with it is when you move a portion of it into a wiser, higher-quality savings vehicle or investment. The money ceases to exist for you except as a growing investment in your freedom and immortality.

To establish your immortality account, begin with the following steps.

Step 1

Figure out how much you make per month, and commit yourself right now to saving 10 percent of every single month's income. That means you'll take it out before you pay for or buy anything else; this has now become your top financial priority, and you're dedicated to honoring it.

Having valued, decided, and committed yourself, go to a financial investment company that offers a full gamut of services and set up a money-market account. This is your immortality account. It will return a safe 2 to 6 percent and will beat inflation so that it will keep growing.

Next, instruct your bank to automatically take 10 percent of your monthly earnings out of your personal account from that day on and deposit it into your immortality account. Why have them do it for you? Because if you had to write a check every month, occasional doubt could sneak in, resulting in about a 60 percent probability that you'd stick to it. At first, most people get excited as they see their wealth grow, and they write that check every month, saying, "Oh yeah! This is fantastic!" Then when they hit the inevitable rough financial month, they get frightened and put it off, and the discipline breaks down. Utilizing automatic withdrawals removes the fear and makes saving a virtual certainty. With automatic withdrawals, the probability goes up to 100 percent that you'll consistently save and invest in yourself— unless, of course, you stop the withdrawal from the bank.

Insurance companies know and use this motivation; that's why they urge you to have your payments automatically withdrawn. They've learned through many years of experience that people who have to write checks drop out 40 percent of the time, while those who utilize automatic deposits stay committed. Don't waver or question or even think about it—just have it done automatically every single month.

Saving 10 percent is a great start, but if it seems like too big a jump, begin with an amount you feel you can handle, then gradually increase it. It's not how much you *make* but how much you *save* that counts, and the *habit* of saving is much more important than the amount you set aside. One man started saving just $8 a month and now he's up to $37. Because he's learned discipline, he'll end up wealthier than the people who say, "When I get something extra, I'll start," and never develop the habit.

You'll get the extra when you start saving, but most people try to do it in reverse. Years ago, I was only paying $1,200 a month to a lady who worked for me, but she worked her way up to saving $400 of it (33 percent), while a colleague I know made $6 million a year and was $200,000 in debt at the end of the year. He made a fortune but saved nothing, while she made much less but saved a lot. What's the difference? He didn't value saving money and therefore didn't know how to manage it.

Money flows to those who demonstrate that they can manage it, and flees from those who don't.

To maximize the effects of this technique for creating wealth, commit to saving a certain percentage or a minimum amount, whichever is greater. For example, decide up front that you're going to save at least $1,000 or 10 percent of your income each month. If 10 percent comes to $1,500, that's how much you save. If it only comes to $900, you still put in $1,000. A minimum amount or a percentage, whichever is greater, is forced out of your account on a certain date by automatic withdrawal—it's guaranteed, without emotion, just paid as an imagined bill. The instant you do that, new money will come in to cover it, because you're making a form of valued commitment. Money is like a relationship: If you don't value it or commit to an outcome, little happens.

Don't beat yourself up if you can't maintain the discipline right off the bat. This is a new approach to money and it can take some time to master. A student of mine came to me recently and said, "Dr. Demartini, when you first told me about your savings program three years ago, I ignored it. I couldn't see how I'd end up with more money by giving myself less to spend. It just seemed like a loss. Then, after almost a year of no growth in my finances, I thought I'd at least give it a try, because what I was doing wasn't working. I saved for three months and then an opportunity for a vacation came along, so I used the money I'd saved to pay for it. I still thought of that money as mine, but it felt a little depressing to suddenly wipe out what I'd been building.

"Afterward, I was more committed and saved for another six months. No luxuries distracted me, and watching my money grow actually became inspiring. But then a whole heap of urgent mortgage, insurance, and car-payment bills came in all at once, and I got scared. I knew the principles by then, but I was just too frightened to trust them and blew my savings again. I was back to zero, and all my efforts seemed defeated, and this time I got really depressed about it. That's when I realized I felt terrible when I allowed my mortal self to spend my soul's wealth, and I finally made a more valued commitment to save *no matter what.*

"That was 18 months ago, and I haven't touched my savings since. It's no longer a hassle or a duty. I get more fulfillment from growing my savings than from almost anything I could buy. I already have *three times* as much money as I've ever had before, and I'm not even sure where it came from. Every time I was tempted to use it but didn't, more money would appear from somewhere else to cover the bills. It's really weird, but it works. For the first time in my life, I believe I'm going to be wealthy. Thank you so much."

That's a perfectly normal scenario for anyone who sets out to master the art of saving money. When you decide to save, you'll be tested, usually three times in different areas of your life. You'll be tested in yourself because you'll be tempted to spend the money on bills or luxuries. Your spouse may suddenly decide to splurge extravagantly, and your business may experience a temporary downturn. It's as if the world is testing you to make sure you're really committed. Pass the test and continue your saving, no matter what. Do this for six to nine months and saving will become a habit. You'll realize that even though you thought you couldn't do it, you can.

*"Experience is a hard teacher because she
gives the test first, the lesson afterward."*

— Vernon Law

When you purchased a new car or leased a better apartment or took out a mortgage on a house, you probably didn't know how you were going to afford it, but somehow you did. Demand creates supply, so put a financial demand on yourself by saving and watch new money become attracted to you from places you never even imagined. If you fail to save, you'll receive lessons to teach you. If you keep saving, you'll get rewards to motivate you. Either way, you'll grow and you can't blow it, so remain encouraged. The only difference is in how long it takes, and as an immortal spirit, you have plenty of time to learn.

Step 2

Having set up your savings program in Step 1, here's another component that will multiply it geometrically, and it's even easier than the first step. Increase your percentage and minimum every three months by 10 percent and watch what happens. That means if you're putting away $1,000 a month, after three months you jump it up by 10 percent and for the next three months you instruct your bank to transfer $1,100. Three months later, you increase it another 10 percent to $1,210, then $1,331, and at the end of a year it rises to $1,464. Then it rises to $1,610, $1,772, $1,949, $2,144, $2,358 . . . it just keeps going up and begins to *accelerate.* You'll be astonished! It doesn't matter if you're saving $1,000 or $100 or $10 a month, the same principle applies. Your wealth will increase proportionately, and you won't notice the increase in deductions.

Research has shown that people can handle financial fluctuations of up to 10 percent without reaction (that's your built-in psychological elasticity), and three months is a reasonable time to allow yourself to adapt to each new level of commitment.

It's important to grow and push yourself to new levels and achievements as you mature. If you aren't growing, don't you feel as if you're stagnant or even going backward? Well, the same principle applies to wealth. Psychologically, you accommodate to the new level in about three months. It becomes natural, and you want to push yourself out of your comfort zone and into a higher one.

Increasing the amount by just 10 percent every quarter will double the sum you save approximately every two years. If you start with $1,000 a month, in two years it will be $2,000, in two more years it will be $4,000, in two more $8,000, and after eight years you'll be saving $16,000 *every month.* You may be thinking, *How the hell am I going to do that on a fixed income? That's more than I make in total!* The answer is that by then you'll probably no longer *be* on a fixed income. Those who commit to this program are seldom on fixed incomes within two to three years. They spontaneously become entrepreneurs who attract new opportunities and make more money than they ever did before.

Fixed incomes lead to fixed lifestyles because of fixed thinking, and this simple program frees up all three. I call it the Forced Acceleration Savings Technique, or FAST for short, and that's the effect it can have on your wealth creation. It's *forced* because you're having it done automatically, so you have reduced emotional attachment and won't interfere. And it's *accelerated* because every three months you kick it up another 10 percent.

There's a principle of economics called the Law of Equilibration, which states that supply and demand equilibrate each other. If you don't increase the demand on yourself, your income and outflow will balance and you'll end up breaking even. When you raise the savings demand, extraordinary things happen. Your goal is to take your savings toward 50 percent of everything you earn, mirroring nature in its equal creation (saving) and destruction (spending). On the day you reach that threshold, your finances will achieve tremendous power and magnetism.

I consulted with a very successful businessman who was making about $500,000 a year and helped him set up a $10,000-a-month forced savings plan. Almost immediately his business and income rose up toward $1 million a year. When we met again a year later and raised his savings to $20,000, his business reached $1.5 million. The next year I asked him how much he thought he could afford to save now. He looked at his wife and she said, "Another $10,000?" That year their business jumped closer to $2 million. The same thing can happen for you on whatever financial level you're currently living. As soon as you value and commit to saving, the universe starts giving you more because you've proved that you can handle it.

Until you manage money wisely, don't expect
more money to manage.

The results are directly proportionate to your commitment. Of the thousands of people I've taken through this technique, those who committed to it are in a completely different financial bracket from their former peers. One young doctor in Canada came to a financial seminar and achieved more than anyone I've ever taught. *Nobody* has ever done so much so fast. He'd been saving $500 a month, and immediately after the seminar he made a solemn commitment to save $10,000. He just said, "The first $10,000 that comes in this month is going into savings, no matter what."

His energy skyrocketed because he created a huge demand *on* himself, and he made a deep commitment that he was determined to do this *for* himself. What he did with his business and finances was simply amazing. He dedicated most of his income to savings, and not only did he hit his target, but more money came in to take care of all his other expenses. He put a large sum of money in his immortality account, paid off his house, bought a new car, and his business just took off. Of course, such a radical strategy is too much for most people, and of the many who've undertaken this challenge, he was certainly one of the higher achievers. By doing what I've described to a high degree, he accelerated his financial freedom. Will you be the one to beat him? Risk and reward are proportionate, and the risk you take in overcoming your fears and committing yourself to follow the universal laws of finance will be exactly equal to the heavenly reward you'll receive.

Dollars and Sense

In the entire history of finance, no one has ever found a single logical reason not to save. The worst thing that can happen is you'll have the money to pay your bills. Of course, the idea is not to spend your savings, but if you need the money, it will be there, so there's no harm in trying. The fear of paying yourself first, probably more than anything else, can prevent you from attaining the heavenly wealth you may desire. *Emotions can destroy wealth, but purposeful strategies can build it.* When you save, you'll receive *more* money to pay your bills, not less.

When I first started saving many years ago, I began with only $200 a month, but it has since grown to over $30,000 and continues to accelerate. My immortality account accumulated rapidly, but not until I valued it, put together a plan, committed to it, and forced my savings. Most people wait to see how much extra they have and then they think about saving some of it. They won't believe it until they see it, and their wealth stays small. The masters declare up front what they're going to save and act as if it has already happened. They believe *before* they see and their wealth becomes great.

The reason the majority can't see the vision is because they're blinded by the false idea, "I have so many bills, I couldn't possibly pay myself first. The expenses have to be covered first." Years of experience have proven that to be untrue and financially unwise. You can continue to pay the costs of living first and keep nothing for yourself, as most people do, but there's an alternative. Pay yourself first, your taxes second, your personal bills third, and your business bills last, and pay them all according to their priorities.

It's wise to pay when services are rendered, but if cash flow dips temporarily, people are patient and can wait for just a short while until cash flow returns. I've had times of low income, but I still pay myself first and don't rob my savings. I just call around to say I have a temporary cash-flow situation and will be paying within 30 days, or I'll pay an additional percentage and guarantee to keep to a payment plan. Do you know how people respond? They say,

"Thank you, that will be fine. Most people don't call us, they just don't pay." Be sure to thank them for believing in you. If you do, they'll appreciate you and extend even more credit because they know they can trust you. Don't let bills interfere with your plan. Of course, after the lull is over, when more money comes in, certainly pay off your bills. But try not to rob your savings to do it.

A long time ago, I began to pay myself with an automatic withdrawal that came out of my account whether I liked it or not. Since that day, my automatic payments have been consistent. Sometimes bills get paid on time and sometimes they're a little late, but my savings and investments have been paid consistently for all those years. I used to pay my bills first and break even without savings. Now I break even or profit *with* my forced savings. I still have my business, and the bills somehow get paid, but now I have guaranteed savings. The secret to making a profit is to take it out first, off the top, in the form of your savings. Declare to the universe, "I'm taking a profit whether my business makes it or not," and guess what happens? You make it. Prioritizing your saving and spending is crucial to growing your heavenly wealth.

The Budget

Preparing a budget can be quite a wake-up call, but it might be just the alarm you need to reprioritize your spending habits. Invest a little time to find out exactly how you spend your income. Add up all your expenditures for a month and multiply by 12 to get the year's total for each of them. You may realize, *My God, I can't believe how much money I spend on low-priority items. Now that I see it, I'm going to shift my values and priorities.*

Spending on lower priorities automatically interferes with your ability to attract more wealth. Spending money on things you don't highly value lowers your self-worth and demonstrates that you're unwisely managing your income. A budget can turn that habit around by motivating you to adjust your spending habits. Most people associate budgeting with deprivation, but when you understand the real value of this simple act, you can embrace and use it to increase your wealth. You'll be grateful once you do.

Discipline

Even with a budget and savings plan in place, there will be a natural ebb and flow to your finances. All of nature rises and falls, and human beings and their incomes and outflows are similar. There will be times when money flows in and times when it dries up a little, but if you allow those ups and downs to run your savings, you'll be back to breaking even again with nothing to show for your work. It's another test of your certainty and commitment. Those who pay themselves first get wealthy. Those who pay themselves last break even or go broke. And those who don't pay themselves at all can end up not only broke but even *destitute,* because inflation can leave them behind and unable to catch up.

You determine your own future by your present actions, so now is a great time to create the heavenly future you'd love. The difference is in how much discipline and patience you have, for these are the qualities of financial maturity. *The greater you value wealth, the more disciplined you'll be.*

Between the person who makes $1,200 a month and saves $400, and the millionaire who saves nothing and descends further into debt, who do you think has the greater financial maturity and the brighter financial future? One values herself and her future and is willing to pass up immediate gratification for long-term and more purposeful objectives. The other lives for the moment like a child, is unable to master either himself or his finances, and dissipates his wealth *and* his life. One moves toward mastery while the other remains a slave, because *long-term gratification makes you money while short-term gratification costs you money.* This means that those who try to get rich quickly usually don't, while those who are methodical and strategic with their savings achieve their grateful and heavenly wealth.

I've made it essential in my business that each of my employees has a savings plan. Nobody gets a raise unless they also increase their savings. At first, some of my employees couldn't see the point and grumbled about interference in their "freedom," but eventually every single one of them thanked me. Why? Because they saw the effects on their lives when financial discipline was imposed upon them. *Very* few people have the self-discipline to become masters of wealth, no matter what their occupation or status. Until you develop the discipline, don't expect the rewards. Once you value wealth, the discipline becomes easy.

I've consulted with many financial brokers, and I've been astonished by how many have little to no personal wealth and how many are actually in debt. They know how to buy and sell, but they haven't learned to save. I worked with some global hedge fund managers in New York and found that, although they had moderate profits, they had little or no savings. They managed vast sums for others but not for themselves. Even though I know how rare mastery is, it was mind-boggling to look behind the scenes into the true financial world. So don't compare yourself to others, and don't be fooled by outer appearances into becoming impatient with your speed of growth. Just stick to the plan that works. In finance, the wise tortoise oftentimes outstrips the foolish hare.

"The haste of a fool is the slowest thing in the world."

— Thomas Shadwell

Money Magnetism

Automatic savings, quarterly acceleration, and budget reprioritization are all powerful and effective strategies for making more profits and building wealth. Yet one magical factor comes into play as your wealth increases: money magnetism. Have you ever noticed that during times when you possessed the most money, additional money flowed more easily to you? *Money acts as a natural magnet and, like gravity, it draws more unto itself as it accumulates.*

The more money you have, the more willing people are to hand over more. The less money you have, the more it's taken away. If you go to the bank and try to borrow $100,000, what does the bank request from you? They request $100,000 worth of collateral. But if you already have that amount of money deposited with them, they ask you if you'd like to borrow from them, even offering special deals because you pose little or no risk. *To those who have, more is given, and from those who haven't, more is taken away.* It's a basic law.

Wealth building is partly a matter of consciousness and resonance. If you save $10, $10 opportunities appear. If you save $100, $100 opportunities appear. Whether you save $1,000, $10,000, or $100,000, that's the size of the opportunities and associates that are magnetically drawn to you by your state of mind. When you reach $1 million, you'll suddenly find you're being offered million-dollar opportunities. It's not so much that you'll be *doing* anything different—you'll *be* different, and you make all the difference in the world.

When you become inspired and infused with life, your business tends to grow. As your business grows and you're filled with life, your money tends to flow. The more you grow and the more money flows, the more others become magnetically drawn to help and share in that inspiration and growth. *Don't spend your life working for money; save money and hire it to work for you.* You'll naturally rise from an emotional and reactive state to a more centered and creative state, and the possibilities you can see for yourself will rise proportionately. That's why it's wise to invest in yourself—to grow and expand your life in every area.

The mastery of money is achieved by the same principles that govern health, relationship, business, or spirituality, because it's *all* spirit. Your wealth and spirit will grow with your savings. The wealthier you become, the more inspiration you'll be able to bring to yourself and others, and the more heaven you'll be able to experience on Earth.

Exercise 1

Start your immortality account. Do it now. Go to your bank or financial institution and commit to it today. Open a special dedicated savings account and instruct the bank to deposit 10 percent of your monthly net income into it from your normal personal or business savings account. (If you're also using the minimum amount option, monitor the amount deposited and up it if necessary.) Then give them the date in three months when they are to raise the deposit by 10 percent of the saved amount, and continue to do it every three months (11 percent, 12.1 percent, 13.3 percent, 14.6 percent, 16 percent, and so on).

There may be a small charge for this service, but what it will do for your commitment and wealth is worth vastly more. Not only will the deposited percentage of your income increase, but demonstrating this level of financial mastery will cause your income to increase as well. Watch it grow, but leave it alone. Remember, *once it goes into this account, imagine that it's no longer yours to spend.* It belongs to your soul, and its long-term purpose is to one day make you more money than you can make by working. This is one of the most powerful steps you'll ever take to begin laying the foundations of your future heavenly wealth. Do it now.

Exercise 2

You have a mortal physical and an immortal spiritual nature. Food and material possessions serve your mortal nature and that's fine, but there's a way to turn them into fuel for your immortal self. Anytime someone takes you out to dinner, or gives you something you already intended to buy, deposit the price of that meal or gift into your immortality account. You were going to spend the money anyway, so now you can give it to your immortal rather than your mortal self. Doing this will increase your awareness of the account, help it grow faster, and make you doubly grateful for whatever you've been given. And because it serves a higher purpose, the number of people offering to pay may inexplicably increase. Try it and you'll see.

Words of Wisdom and Power

- *I pay myself first, no matter what.*

- *I take the cream off the top, because I'm worth it.*

- *My disciplined savings plan adds to the wealth of my immortal spirit.*

- *I am a master of money, and money works for me.*

- *I manage money wisely, so I attract ever more money to manage.*

- *I am a money magnet, and money flows to me from the most amazing places.*

Chapter Six

Manage Your Emotions . . . or They'll Manage You

*"Until you can manage your emotions,
don't expect to be able to manage money."*

— Warren Buffett

SO WHAT the hell are emotions anyway, and what do they have to do with creating heavenly wealth? To answer these questions, let's return to a little physics. We explored three profound principles in Chapter 1:

1. The universe is filled with light energy or spirit.

2. Matter is like light frozen at lower frequencies.

3. Your true spiritual essence is divine light and love, not in the common understanding of the words, but rather in a state of unshakable *presence,* the still point in the midst of movement.

Photons, or energy particles of light, can convert into dense particles of matter by splitting into positively charged positrons and negatively charged electrons. Together they store as much energy as the original light particles, but the energy is converted into opposing complementary particles of matter. These positively and negatively charged particles attract and repel other charged particles around them.

As far as you're concerned, this light energy represents your loving presence, and those complementary particles of material represent your positive and negative emotions. Like positrons and electrons, emotions come in pairs, with lots of expressed energy but little illumination.

Every time you enter an emotional state, you split the light and power of your true nature into positive elation and negative depression. That's why love and light are truth, and emotions are only half-truths. Anything you have an emotion about runs your life and in some sense robs you of your ability to manifest your dreams. When you're elated, you'll recklessly squander time and money. When you're depressed, you'll hoard your resources. Both extremes cause wealth to flee from you because you simply can't manage money wisely while in these states. You have the capacity to do what you love and receive great wealth in doing it, but until you master your emotions, you won't master your life or your finances. When you integrate these two extreme states, your wealth becomes possible once again. Emotions dissipate consciousness and wealth, while grateful and loving presence builds them.

Science has demonstrated that when two complementary charged particles of matter are reunited, they disappear and light is birthed once again. You're made of light, so the same princi-ples apply to you. When reunited in perfect balance, your dense emotions disappear and you return to your original divine nature. Here the light of love is reborn. Emotions represent scattered energy, but love represents focused presence. That loving pres-ence is where your heavenly power lies. It only arises in a state of balanced emotion. When you're lovingly present, you act with intent as a creator and are certain. When you're fragmented with emotions, you react with fear as a creature. You're in financial bondage when you're emotional, and you're free when you're in truth. To the degree that you master your emotions, you move from creature to creator and are able to manifest wealth at will.

Those are a few of the universal principles. Now let's explore how they function in your daily world.

"Love has power to give in a moment what toil
can scarcely reach in an age."

— Johann Wolfgang von Goethe

Emotion, Not Love, Is Blind

The nature of your worldly existence is duality. Everything shares in this dual nature of positive and negative, making up a perfect equilibrium. For every elation, there's a depression; for every infatuation, a resentment; for every rise, a fall. When you see both sides simultaneously, you enter into the powerful state of grateful spirit. But whenever you see only one side of any person, idea, or event, you experience half-powered emotions. Emotions are due to lopsided perceptions of a balanced world, and they'll persist until *you* return to balance. A positive emotion is triggered by anything you're attracted to, and a negative emotion by anything you're repelled by, and both will run you if you let them.

You see few if any drawbacks when you're infatuated, and you see few if any benefits when you're resentful, because emotions blind you to the other side. They automatically make you see more positives than negatives, or vice versa, and cause you to react and invest unwisely. Until someone labels them as good or bad, all events are neutral because they have both sides in equilibrium. If you have no liquid capital but lots of investments and the stock market goes up, you'll think, *Great, I'm really making money here!* But someone with a lot of liquidity could watch the market rise and think it was a catastrophe. Stock-market fluctuations are due far more to the emotions of investors than to the worth of the shares, and commonly the higher the booms, the lower the busts that follow.

The gurus of the financial markets are those who've learned to master their own emotions, but most people lose money because they let their emotions dictate their behavior. Emotions impair judgment, so emotional people buy when they're elated and sell when they're fearful or depressed, and pay the price. With wisdom, you can make profits no matter what the market does. The rise and fall of markets is completely neutral until you impose your illusions of good and bad on it, and the same thing applies to people.

> *"Good is when I steal other people's wives and cattle; bad is when they steal mine."*
>
> — Hottentot proverb

Until you learn the art of mastering your emotions at whatever level you've reached, don't expect more opportunities for financial growth to come to you. And until you learn the art of managing money wisely, don't expect more money to come into your hands. Why would the world give you more of *anything* when you can't manage what you already have? If you try to give people promotions before they've developed the skills and talents to do the job, it usually backfires, doesn't it? Promotions go to people who know how to handle them, and so does money. Emotional extremes create personal and financial chaos, while calm certainty sees and creates order. The more you know how to stay centered and work moderately with whatever happens, the more leadership opportunities and wealth will come to you.

People who are run by their emotions are uncertain and inevitably become followers to those with greater certainty.

Emotions are created and fueled by the illusion of an imbalanced world—the belief that it's possible to have positive without negative, gain without loss, pleasure without pain. This type of thinking attracts a lesson. Whatever you try to run away from you run into, and whatever you try to bury buries you, until you learn to love both sides. Any part of your life, any person, place, thing, idea, or event that you try to avoid or seek runs your life. But anything you see both sides of you can love and manage. You are the master of what you love and the slave to what you don't.

". . . Excessive pains and pleasures are justly to be regarded as the greatest disease to which the soul is liable. For a man who is in great joy or in great pain, in his unseasonable eagerness to attain the one and avoid the other, is not able to see or hear anything right; he is mad, and is at the time utterly incapable of any participation in reason."

— Plato

I once consulted with a wealthy, middle-aged gentleman in New York who had left a long-term relationship with a woman his own age to run off with a girl 20 years younger. Even though they'd been through so much together, in his mind he saw the older woman as loaded with negatives, and he couldn't wait to get away from her. Because of the abrupt way he ended his relationship to follow his illusion, he elicited such resentment that he lost business contacts. He didn't care, though, because he was totally infatuated with the younger woman. All he could see was a beautiful, sexy, exciting girl full of positives.

He took her off to a Caribbean island and bought a big fancy convertible to ride around and show her off in. Although he hadn't exercised in years, he started bicycling and scuba diving, and stayed up late most nights drinking and partying with his new fantasy love. Everything seemed like paradise, but after a brief period of intoxication, the other side inevitably appeared: He developed lung damage and sexual-performance problems, he neglected his business to the point where it accumulated grow-ing liabilities and debts, and he blew a whole lot of his saved money. He was also stressed because he couldn't keep up with the younger woman and was afraid she'd run off with some young stud, just as he'd done to his previous partner.

Because he'd been infatuated with the girl and imagined she had more positives than negatives, he ended up having to deal with all the negatives later. By fleeing age and following youth, he ended up feeling even older. That isn't to say a loving relation-ship wasn't possible, but he was run by his passionate emotions rather than being guided wisely by his loving heart. He thought he could break the laws of the universe and get all the pleasure without any of the pain, but his infatuation cost him in every other area of his life. The higher the cost became, the better his old rela-tionship started to look to him. If only he'd known the truth of balance and had trained himself to look for it, he could have saved himself a lot of heartache and wealth.

It's simple physics. For every positive in the universe, there's a negative, and when they're joined together, the power of love and light is reborn. When you know that every positive event in life has a concealed drawback, and every negative event has a hidden benefit, outside financial circumstances lose their power to elate or depress you. On the day you truly understand this, you'll take a giant stride toward manifesting your fortune, but until then, you'll get emotional and financial lessons to teach it to you. The only time you're truly free is in the moment you find the divine Law of Equilibrium. When you see perfect balance all around you, you become liberated because you know that you can neither gain nor lose, and you act with inner certainty and heavenly appreciation.

The Coiled Spring

The key to growing wealth and worth is emotional stability, and here's a simple analogy that explains why: Life is like an infi-nite spring coiling continuously 'round and 'round, always rising to ever higher levels. You walk the journey of your life along that springy coil, and as long as it holds steady, it's easy to keep going. But when you get elated, the spring bobs up; and when you get depressed, it bobs down. When it's bobbing up or down, it becomes unstable and you have to stop and hold on.

Attempting to make your way up the road toward wealth is just like trying to walk up the coiled spring. There will be times when you're bobbing up or riding high, and others when you're bobbing down or riding low. There will be times when you get frantic about your economic growth and curl into a fetal position. Emotional highs and lows make it difficult to follow your journey. They distract you from your chief aim and force you to stop. The path is actually your own mind, and you only get to walk along it when you're stabilized.

Taken a step further, here's how this internal bobbing manifests itself on an even larger scale throughout the physical world. Whenever the population of a nation, state, or city becomes cocky and overvalues itself (bobbing high), it automatically attracts neutralizing catastrophic events to humble it. When a real estate market becomes hyperinflated and masses of people are buying in and saying, "Buy real estate; you can't lose, everybody's going to make a fortune!" that elated mass consciousness attracts geological, meteorological, and social calamities to bring it back into equilibrium. As the Bible says, pride goes before the fall, and every mountain is leveled and every valley is filled. Whole cities experience earthquakes, fires, storms, floods, or social upheavals when their citizens lose mental equilibrium on a large enough scale. It represents a form of collective social consciousness.

In Los Angeles, California, in the early '90s, the real estate market was overinflated, and that city attracted floods, fires, earthquakes, mudslides, riots—and massive property damage. Afterward, there was a major correction and a return to realistic values. In other words, they learned their lesson and things calmed down. Florida experienced similar problems in the 1930s. The principle has been consistent around the world: If you allow yourself to get elated, you force yourself into depression.

On a personal level, emotions also create chaos. Say you're at home and everything's a total mess. Your hair's in rollers, you need a bath, the kitchen's filthy, and the house looks like a family of baboons has moved in. Suddenly the phone rings and the best friend you haven't seen in five years is on the line: "Hi! I'm just around the corner with my new husband. Can we stop by?" You can't say no because that makes no sense, but you don't want to say yes because, "Oh my God, look at this place!" You fear what they'll think of you when they see the squalor you're temporarily surrounded by, but you really want to see your friend. Your dualistic emotions put you in an either-or situation, so you do one of two things: Either you throw your hands in the air and go back to bed, pulling the covers over your head while you lie there in a fetal position, or you frantically race around trying to fix everything in two minutes (even though it's impossible), and stall answering the door.

When your emotions put you in an either-or situation, it seems that for someone to win, somebody else has to lose. That creates a paradox, and the only way to successfully resolve a paradox is to rise above it with greater clarity and certainty into the higher perspective I call a "metadox." A metadox goes beyond or transcends the two contrary sides of a paradox; it's a transcendent synthesis of the thesis and antithesis.

Whenever you're faced with a decision, stop and breathe for a moment. Then realize you have four choices for all decisions: this, that, both, or neither. You can choose one option or the other, find a way to combine both, or even choose neither of them. Believing only in a "this or that" solution can stalemate you. But if you don't lock yourself in, sometimes a totally new alternative arises in your mind. The master is the one who can sit in the center and choose. The highest levels of the brain have the greatest number of options, and so does the leader in any given situation. It's this form of certainty and freedom that leads to great heavenly wealth.

The Cushion

Emotions can make you do too much or too little of some activity, and in the financial world, doing too much or too little doesn't just stress you, it perceptibly costs you time and money. So, how do you manage your financial emotions and neutralize these calamitous extremes? The key is not to get elated if you make money and not to get depressed if you don't. What helps you create that stability is the ever-growing base of your immortality account, which I call the reserve or cushion portion of your account. A cushion is designed to free you up to live your dreams, to moderate and neutralize your emotions so your wealth and business can grow. Throughout your life, your wealth will grow from tens of dollars to hundreds, to thousands, to tens of thousands, to hundreds of thousands, to millions, and each new level will initiate a new elation or depression until you learn to stabilize yourself at the new, more expanded level. The growing cushion helps you do this at each new level.

Let's say you have a business that makes $1,000 a day. If you suddenly have a $5,000 day, you're very likely to get elated and start manically imagining a future of fabulous wealth. If you have a $20 day, you'll probably get depressed and start to imagine disaster: *Oh my god, if things go on like this, I'll be bankrupt soon!* You keep imagining zoom or doom proportionate to the degree of rise or fall, and both emotional extremes dilute your ability to manage your business and your money.

The best defense against this normal human reaction is a sizable cushion. Your goal here is to set up a cushion account and keep making deposits into it, even if it's only $50 a week, until it has enough money to cover at least two months of your earnings. For example, if you make $500 a day and work 20 days a month, you'll need $20,000 to cover two months.

Again, this is not for spending, it's just there to help keep you centered. The larger the amount in your cushion, the greater the centering effect. It's a base of liquid money that you put into a safe bank or money-market account and don't touch, and you keep building it until it contains at least two months' worth of your income. With this cushion in place, you'll be less reactive and more able to stay centered and follow the wealth-building principles. If you make money, you won't get too elated because it's only a small percentage of what you already have; and if you lose money, you won't get too depressed because you have enough to keep going without too much distraction.

I presented my first course on financial mastery some years ago to a group of doctors, and I recently followed up with some of them to see how they were doing. Those who followed these techniques have tripled and quadrupled their net worth and have grown their businesses. It's amazing what has happened, and this can be your future, too, if you do the same.

When you begin to manage money wisely, you get more money to manage, so make sure you increase the cushion proportionately as your income rises. When your income doubles to $1,000 a day, double the cushion to $40,000 to match it. With that reserve in place, your highs and lows will stabilize, the money will earn interest, and you'll have the confidence of greater financial security. You'll be less likely to react with a child's extreme emotions, and your finances will grow and mature.

For the Love of Money

In a wedding ceremony, the profound vows of love state, "For better, for worse, for richer, for poorer, in sickness, and in health." That means you love your spouse for both sides of life. But if you imagine wealth to be one-sided pleasure and happiness, you're living in an elated fantasy and you may be shocked and resentful when the other side shows up. If you don't love money, which means to embrace both its pleasure and its pain, it will continue to elude you and run your life. Understand that money won't make you happy; everything in life just changes the form of your pleasures and pains and comes with a price. When you're willing to pay the price, you've earned the reward.

> *"I find this wealth a terrible burden,*
> *and I would trade it all for one successful relationship."*
>
> — J. Paul Getty

What are some of the prices that come with wealth? As it grows, it can consume ever more of your time, taking you away from loved ones and pastimes, and making it increasingly difficult for you to take a moment to walk in nature or just relax. It can bring increasing responsibilities over what to do with it, where to invest it, and with whom. The size of your risks increases, and every decision carries the possibility of setbacks. You may alienate or even transform friends and relatives, and people or charities looking for handouts are drawn to you like flies after honey. You must monitor and track all of your investments, or they could become reduced in a very short time. You might create resentful envy and become a target—a "tall poppy," as they say in Australia, someone who rises above the average and gets cut down or attacked by anyone who feels they have less than you.

The government may watch you like a hawk, with all its audits, penalties, and fines. You or your children or partner could become the target of kidnappers, and you may even require security guards, bringing more costs and restrictions. You may no longer be sure if your friends and loved ones truly *are* your friends and loved ones, or if they're merely attracted to your money. If you no longer needed to work and hadn't found a mission to dedicate your life to, you could become unmotivated, isolated, or disheartened. Your health could be impacted by the stress of all these new conditions. Unless you've achieved a degree of gratitude and self-mastery, you could indulge in personal excesses when you're no longer restrained by limiting options and power.

If you haven't matured enough to handle the great power and responsibility that come with great wealth, you might impact yourself and others. The wealthy can behave in ways you're unlikely to hear about until you become one of them. A very wealthy friend was out jogging one morning and passed by the window of an exclusive men's clothing store. He trotted in and asked to see their finest suits. The clerk took one look at the man in his shorts and T-shirt and, with his most condescending sneer, said, "Sir, I think the clothes *you* would be looking for are over here," and directed him to the cheaper clothes near the back. After listening to a few more calculated insults and slights, my friend became so infuriated that he asked to see the owner and requested to buy the store on the spot. Upon negotiating an outrageously high purchase price, he insisted that the supercilious clerk be fired. He allowed his emotions free rein because he had the financial power, but the satisfaction was only temporary because he soon became distracted and guilty about what he wanted to do to the salesman. It cost him time and energy in the long run.

Money brings both pain and pleasure, and unless you master your emotions, those pleasures and pains can be very intense. Without inner balance, emotions can make great wealth into a hell rather than the heaven you imagine will automatically come with it. Heaven is a state of mind, and you glimpse it every moment you come to the center with gratitude. Emotions come from the mortal self and are located in the head. Love comes from the immortal self and is centered in the heart. The love of heaven, and the power to create and have what you love, comes to you when you're in your heart, in balance.

"The mind is its own place, and in itself
Can make a Heaven of Hell, a Hell of Heaven."

— John Milton

The Four Cardinal Pillars

Four magical human qualities—gratitude, love, certainty, and presence—make up the four cardinal pillars of the temple of your true inspired and awakened mind. The first two, gratitude and love, are qualities of the heart. The last two, certainty and presence, are qualities of the mind.

Whenever you bring these emotions into balance, you become grateful, you feel love in your heart, you have a certainty that can't be shaken, and you exude the power of tremendous presence. You can trust the power of these four qualities and their magical ability to utterly transform any circumstances in your life.

They give you the power to overcome obstacles, while emotional extremes merely lead to excuses.

When these emotions occur simultaneously, you experience divine equilibrium, which is the will of God. When your human will matches divine will, you evolve and grow to ever greater levels of ability and worth. The instant you deny that equilibrium, you create unbalanced emotions, become disempowered, and struggle in a battle you can't win. When you're divided against yourself, your emotions keep you from doing what you love and building your heavenly wealth. The more grateful you are, the more you integrate your force and power. The more ungrateful you are, the more you *dis*integrate.

Two months after I opened my first chiropractic practice, everything started to nosedive. Client numbers fell through the floor, and I became alarmed.

I called up a buddy and said, "My practice is bombing, and I don't know why. Is yours up or down?"

He said, "It's way down. I guess it's just Christmastime."

I called another colleague, then another . . . I called seven young chiropractors, and they all said the same thing. I began to believe this was just what happens to doctors at Christmas and there was nothing I could do about it. States of mind are states of vibration, and that was the vibrational consciousness I resonated with when I was down and frightened. But I made one more call to another friend, and when I asked to speak to him, his receptionist said, "Can you hold on? He's with a patient." As I waited on the line, I could hear that it was very loud, and business was booming in his office. He saw nearly 200 patients a day, and it sounded as if they were all there at once.

When he came to the phone, I asked him how things were going and he said, "Whoo! Man, it's unbelievable. It seems like everybody in the world wants to come in before Christmas. How is it with you?"

"Oh, I just wanted to see how you were doing."

"Oops, I have to go, people are backing up here. Talk to you later," and *Poof!* he was gone.

When I hung up, I thought, *Damn, why did I have to call him?* Before that call, I had an excuse for why things weren't going so well. But I'd noticed on the phone that he demonstrated a powerful and sincere love for his patients, while I was self-absorbed; he was inspired, while I was uninspired; he was certain, while I was full of doubt; he was present, while I was scattered and focused on excuses.

What a lesson I learned. He was following the principles that built wealth and business. He was grateful and loving and certain and present. He was booming. He reminded me at that moment to do the same, so I became humbled, focused, and present with my business instead of looking for excuses and blaming forces outside myself. I became very clear on what I desired to have happen instead of dwelling on what I feared might happen. I broke through my scattering emotions and returned to my heart, and my business zoomed before Christmas and just kept rising. It wasn't the economy or the people or the holidays or anything else—it was me! When I got reinspired, the business came back.

Researchers at the Institute of HeartMath in Boulder Creek, California, conduct experiments on the capacities of the human mind in different states of consciousness. They've found that when people attain the states of gratitude and love, and when their brains and hearts enter into a state of coherence, the power of their intent and presence is maximized. Subjects in this state of loving presence were able to impact strands of DNA in a beaker some distance away, *just by willing it to happen.* Likewise, you have the ability to affect matter and change the world around you with your mind. The most powerful states of heart and mind available to human beings are ones of gratitude, love, certainty, and presence.

Emotions are fleeting, but love is eternal, and the more you can be in this enlightened state, the more brightly your light will shine. You either give off light or you take it in. If you take in light, the world rules you. If you give off light, you govern the world. Know that there's nothing but love and all else is illusion—that *is* the "kingdom of heaven," and in that state nothing you love will be denied you. Moderate your emotions to reconnect with the light of your spirit, and gain the patience and certainty to apply the financial principles you're learning here. When you've mastered your emotions, you'll master money, and wealth will flow to you because you've earned the right to manage it.

Exercise

Here's a great way to moderate your financial emotions and increase your money magnetism. Decide how much you'd love to make in a day, and simply start carrying that amount in your wallet. You won't fully comprehend the power of this step until you take it. If you want to make $1,000 a day, carry $1,000. If you want to make $10,000, carry *that.*

Don't spend this money. It's purely a psychological cushion, so put it in a separate section of your wallet, away from your spending money. Not only will this create stability and confidence, it's also a powerful money magnet. When you get used to carrying that amount, it becomes normal to you, and you begin to resonate with it and believe you deserve it.

The psychology of this exercise is that you're a car and the money is your tank. When you're driving in your car and the gas tank is almost empty, doesn't that affect your state of mind? You're more likely to be anxious and worried about running out of gas and distracted from your driving. To have no money in your pocket is like driving on empty, while carrying a wallet stuffed with $10,000 feels entirely different. One sets you up to feel emotionally vulnerable, and the other adds to your confidence. It's a game of consciousness, so take advantage of it.

There's an old saying: When thy purse is full, more enters thy purse. Some people say they'd be afraid to lose so much money, but I have yet to see it happen. However, the fear of losing any amount can also interfere with manifesting it, so don't allow yourself to hang on to this fear. Besides, if you're afraid of "losing" a day's earnings, you're not following the principles. When you have a reserve built up, the loss of one day's pay is insignificant.

One more thing. Carrying cash is entirely different from having a credit card. Cash is like a psychological interest-bearing account, an investment in certainty. Carrying as much as you'd love to make in a day stabilizes your money at that level, and the certainty you gain from it will make you far more money than the 4-percent interest a bank would return.

Empty pockets cost you money; full pockets make you money. Money is a vibration, so carry it and raise yours.

Words of Wisdom and Power

- *I transcend the illusions of emotional pain and pleasure with financial wisdom.*

- *Elusive emotions cost money. True, loving presence builds wealth.*

- *I use the power of silence in order to be heard.*

- *I have the power to choose this, that, both, or neither.*

- *I remain centered and let neither elation nor depression distract me.*

- *Great wealth brings great responsibilities, so I embrace both.*

- *My balanced heart and mind bring me financial freedom.*

Chapter Seven
Evolutionary Investing

"The stock market is a financial redistribution system.
It takes money away from those who have no patience
and gives it to those who have."

— Warren Buffett

SO FAR, you've come a long way and learned a great deal. You've discovered that wealth is only another aspect of divinity, you've seen the importance of maintaining fair exchange in all your affairs, you've explored the power of appreciation and gratitude, and you've realized the importance of honoring yourself as well as others. I hope you've set up your immortality or cushion account, begun moderating your emotions, and started carrying as much money as you'd love to make in a day. If you diligently follow all these principles, your heavenly wealth will begin to increase, first slowly and then exponentially. So what are you supposed to do with all this wealth? How do you keep and increase it? That's what this chapter is all about.

Let's start by reframing what money really is. One of the earliest forms of money was cattle. In humankind's earliest history, livestock was wealth. That worked well within small communities, but as cultures grew it became inconvenient and difficult to drive the cattle across great distances. People had to find a more efficient way, so when the smelting of metal began, they made coins that were portable and durable. The word *capital* actually comes from the Latin *caput,* meaning "head," and the earliest coins bore the image of a cow's head.

As wealth increased along with the size and distance of transactions, coins became too heavy and inefficient to carry, so paper money was added. Soon, letters of credit appeared on the scene to represent large amounts of paper money, then credit cards that were even lighter and more secure. Most recently, we've witnessed the development of electronic and Internet banking, where vast sums of money can be moved around the world at the push of a button. A financial evolution has occurred, a gradual refinement from flesh to metal to paper to plastic to electromagnetic energy, from very slow and dense to very fast and light. In fact, with electromagnetic transfers, money has literally become a form of light.

Just as wealth has undergone an evolution of its form, consciousness has also evolved from the concrete to the abstract, from dense matter to rarefied spirit. Money and consciousness are both evolving together, demonstrating an important principle of life: Nature does not throw away old mechanisms; it just builds new ones on top of what has proven successful.

As an unborn baby still in the womb, you partially recapped the evolution of all lower life forms, growing from a unicellular creature to an amphibian with little gills, passing through all the stages from reptilian to mammalian to human before you were born. This is nature's way of ensuring growth and development, and you would be wise to do exactly the same with the wealth you create. Some of the most magnificent and enduring human-made structures on Earth are the great pyramids of Egypt, which were also created level by level. You've already begun learning a similar program for building wealth: building a financial pyramid on a stable base with little or no risk, rising through a series of graduated evolutionary stages as your resources and skills increase, and ultimately rising to a peak of knowledge and wealth.

The Base

You may not have been aware of it, but if you've set up your immortality or cushion account, you've already laid the foundation for your financial pyramid. Your cushion account, as you learned in the last chapter, should hold an amount equal to at least 60 days of your income. If you make $10,000 a month, that's a base of $20,000. Automatically deposit your selected amount or percentage, whichever is greater, into a money-market savings account. Even though at first it may only attract a safe 3 to 6 percent interest, this minimal amount will become the bedrock of your financial structure. It's meant to be slow and stable, like the solid earth.

Your cushion account makes up the foundation upon which your wealth will be built, and unless the foundation is in place, your structure won't stand. Would you agree that if you tried to run before you could walk, or walk before you could crawl, you'd encounter difficulties and setbacks? Financial development is similar. If you try to jump ahead of your true level of knowledge and financial risk tolerance, you'll probably end up falling back to it and dissipating your money.

Some people think, *Yeah, but I could get into the stock market and make a hell of a lot more even quicker.* It's more important to save and build emotional stability and security; investing comes later. I know many people who jumped into high-risk investments a few years ago, and they watched a *pot* of money disappear because they had no base. Build your heavenly wealth as I instruct, and you'll end up making far more money in your business and life by being stable than what the interest difference could bring you on a higher-yielding investment. It doesn't matter if it takes a year or two. Just add to your savings account every month. Grow your savings until you earn the right to risk. Build a foundation of heavenly wealth first. This gives you time to practice managing or balancing your emotions anyway.

Most people try to get into investments before they've earned the right to be there. They try to run and soar before they've even crawled. A few years ago, I consulted with some financial advisers from one of the world's top brokerage houses. When I introduced them to this strategy, some of them said, "Six percent? No way! What about all the money we could be making for our clients with that cash?"

I said, "No, what you'd have is people initially making money who'd get elated and cocky and couldn't manage it. Then when the market drops, they'd react by pulling all their money out and going back to zero again." They admitted that was exactly what was happening.

Without a base, their investors weren't emotionally stable enough to handle the fluctuations of the market. In addition, the financial brokers didn't know how to deal with their clients' responses. Their clients were elated at the thought of making a killing. They said they could handle the risk ratio and emotions, but they couldn't. When their shares crashed, they panicked and sold at a loss, and it cost the company a fortune as investors dropped out of the market.

Eventually my message got through, and this major firm is now reeducating some of their people to strategize and methodically follow a plan to develop financial cushions. Their goal is no longer to make a killing, but to make sure their clients earn the right to earn money, because they know they'll all be wealthier in the long run. If building a cushion is wise enough for the world's leading financiers, it's probably wise enough for you.

The Pyramid

Once the base is filled with two months' worth of your income as pure liquid capital, safe and stable, you're ready to stair-step it up to the next level. Like nature, you don't throw the old base away. You just build a new one on top of it that reaches even higher.

The second level of your financial pyramid should earn a slightly higher interest rate, so start putting your money into selective, highly rated municipal bonds or treasury bills that will yield 5 to 7 percent over time. These investments are a little less liquid and offer a higher return than your cushion account, but no great risk is involved. After all, when children learn to walk, they don't practice on the highway. Keep making deposits at this level until you reach the same $20,000 total (or whatever two months' income is for you).

When that level is full, you move up to the next one and start making your automatic deposits there. The third level of your pyramid will now contain a balanced mutual fund and index fund (mostly corporate bonds and a few blue-chip stocks) that will return you 7 to 9 percent over time. This is your first level of actual investment; everything else up until now has been a form of savings with proportionately low risks and returns. Once again, you'll build the same two months' worth of capital before going on to the next level.

At the fourth level, begin buying shares of purely blue-chip stocks, which are large-capitalized, name-brand companies with lots of capital and long-term stability. Buy mutual funds or index funds that are spread across many or most sectors of the blue-chip market. These will probably yield 9 to 11 percent over time. Again, another $20,000 (or two months' worth of income) goes here before you move up.

The next layer is made up of mid- to large-cap stocks at 11 to 13 percent. These companies are not as well known and/or are a little more volatile, but by this time you've earned the right to play in that level of the game. Besides, it will only be a small to moderate percentage of your total portfolio.

Then comes the next level of your financial pyramid, where you'll be dealing with mid- and small-cap stocks and maybe even warrants, options, and (later on) hedge funds that may yield larger interest rates with proportionately higher risks. These are more speculative and specialized forms of economic exchange, and you wouldn't be wise to try your hand at them until you've worked through all the levels below. Taking higher risks is an earned right, because by the time you get to that level, you'll know a hell of a lot more about the art of managing your money.

When a level is full, leave it alone and go on to the next, but allow the interest in each one to accumulate there. Structuring your finances in this way increases the probability of not only growth at each level, but also an increase in your earnings.

Review your finances annually and "top up" each level by real-locating your money to match two months (or more) of your increasing income. The first level may seem to take quite a long time to build, but successive layers will be filled progressively faster for several reasons:

1. Each level attracts a higher level of interest that will be compounded because you're leaving it there.

2. As your wealth increases, you become more emotionally stable and grateful. Wealth grows like a living entity, and just as you do with your children, you appreciate it more as it grows and develops. Whatever is appreciated appreciates.

3. Increasing wealth acts like a magnet. More money and opportunities come to you because of your new level of resonance. The more you deposit into your pyramid of wealth, the more you'll receive to add to it. You're like a rocket leaving the earth—the higher you go, the faster you rise. As gravity decreases, the density of the atmosphere lessens and momentum builds.

Each stage of your financial pyramid is not only a stair step, it's also an added cushion. As your capital increases, you can afford to take more risk and receive a higher return. You're not just increasing your wealth, you're building your self-worth and increasing your emotional ability to handle greater risk. When you can handle a challenge with certainty, you get an entirely different outcome. People without these cushions leap into the risky stock market and go *up* . . . and then often come *down.* They crash, and their wealth and business fall with them. Don't try to get rich quick. It's a recipe for getting poor fast.

"When you are emotional, you make unwise decisions rapidly."
— Warren Buffett

A few years ago, one of my client's apartments burned down and she received an insurance payout of $80,000. She came to me and asked, "What do you think I should do with all this money?" As I opened my mouth to answer, she blurted out, "A friend said I should put it all into this hot stock he's heard about."

I said, "Lisa, I would strongly advise against it."

"What! Why? It's really on a *roll.*"

I answered, "First off, you're talking about almost all of the money you presently have. You have little other cash reserve, no other investments, and no knowledge of either the market or this particular stock. On that basis alone, you're unwise to put all your money into such a speculation. You'll have too high a chance of saying good-bye to your money."

"But, but . . . it just seems too good to pass up. I could make a fortune," Lisa argued.

"Even if it earned a pile of money," I replied, "it could still cost you. You'd think your friend was a genius, or that you were really lucky, or that the stock market is easy, and next time you got a tip you'd plunge into that one. Once again, you'd have a high chance of saying good-bye to your money. I know you're not prepared to lose even what you have now, and that could really crush you. Believe me, I've seen people face this many times."

"Oh, darn it. All right, what do *you* think I should do?"

Lisa was generally a smart woman, and even though she was a financial novice, she had the sense to consult with someone who knew more about finances than she did. She was also wise enough to follow the advice she was given. I sensed that if she didn't do something conservative with her money, she might act on her stock tip, so I advised her to leave some of her money liquid in a money-market account and a little in bonds and large-cap stocks.

It just so happened that if she had put her entire $80,000 into that stock, it would be worth $43,000 today. She would have had a setback of $37,000 and could not have handled throwing away nearly 50 percent of her wealth. The financially immature get elated about making money quickly and resentful about saying good-bye to it the same way.

If you follow this tried-and-true plan, you'll end up with a multilevel savings and investment portfolio, a stable pyramid of increasing wealth with moderate returns and certainty. Your financial knowledge will also increase through experience and association with those who know the financial world, and one day you'll be surprised to find that you've become one of them and that people are coming to you for advice. Keep building your cash base and reserve, stabilize your emotions, and follow the strategy, and you'll end up far wealthier than those who try to make a quick killing. You don't raise a child or a fortune overnight. Have the wisdom of patience. Follow a slow, methodical strategy. It's one of the secrets of manifesting heavenly profits and true financial fulfillment. The greater your cushions, the greater your returns will be.

"To know and to act are one and the same."

— Wang Yang-ming, Chinese philosopher

That's the basic plan. It's simple but effective. When it begins to take effect, you'll attract more money than you've ever had before.

Now let's look at some finer points of how to manage your wealth.

Beginner's Mind

Those who manage money wisely will receive more money to manage. Now, you may not feel wise yet, and some of the concepts and terms may be unfamiliar to you, but don't worry. That's *perfect,* because you're a beginner with an open mind and no preconceptions to deter you from the path of financial wisdom. You have plenty of time to become accustomed to each level and learn about the next one before you reach it.

Once you begin to understand the principles laid out here and see the big picture, you can get all the information you need about the details. Simply call an investment house or stockbroker in your city, tell them you want to start creating a stair-stepped investment portfolio, and they'll probably be delighted to sit down with you and explain the process. They can translate any terms you don't understand and recommend investments appropriate to each of the levels you'll be working on.

When you wish to invest, you'd be wise to consult several advisers from different companies to attain a balanced perspective and locate someone you can trust. Financial investment advisers or brokers also offer seminars on money and investment, many of them free, so take advantage of these opportunities. Knowledge is power.

Dodos

In nature, overspecialization can lead to extinction. Because the dodo bird was confined to one island, it easily became extinct. In Australia, koala bears feed on just one type of eucalyptus leaf; they can't move around, and if the trees die or are cut down, the koalas don't make it. Learn from nature, and don't put all your eggs in one basket.

The plan outlined in this book describes multiple levels of savings and investments, and you'd be wise to diversify each of those levels into many sectors or sections. This especially applies when you reach the third level of 7 to 9 percent and beyond. I studied the lives of 12 billionaires and found that their investments were well diversified. They didn't have too many or too few, although they had "pets" that they focused on and cared about. You can break a single pencil with just two fingers, but if you have eight or nine pencils, you can't break them at all, even using both hands. So consider how many pencils you have in your financial house. If you put all your money into one investment, you can easily experience a setback. Make your structure stable. With some diversification, you won't be broken. The decreases in one section will be more than equaled by the increases in the others, so your portfolio stays stable and your pyramid keeps growing.

Resonance

As your heavenly wealth grows, you're naturally going to require people to manage it for you, and you want to be able to trust them. Here are some simple rules to help you with that.

Don't give your money to any individual or company that has less than you do, because anyone who doesn't know how to manage money usually has it taken away and given to those who do. For example, if you put a $1 million health practitioner into a $100,000 practice, that practice will soon go up to $1 million. But if you give a $1 million practice to a $100,000 practitioner, it will soon drop to $100,000 because that's the level of consciousness at which the practitioner resonates. It's not so much the business that creates the wealth, it's the consciousness and skills of the practitioner.

If you give money to someone who vibrates lower than you do, watch how quickly that money will disappear out of their hands, because they don't know how to manage it. Invest your money uphill to greater expertise and certainty, not downhill. If you have $1 million, consider investing it with someone who has $10 million because they've been where you are and know how to get to the next level. If they don't know, they'll be on a learning curve, they'll probably blow it, and you'll pay the price of their education. Find someone who knows how to manage your money more wisely than you do, and go uphill with your wealth.

Optimists and Pessimists

When choosing financial planners or advisers to help you fulfill your savings and investment strategies, I recommend that you have not one but two: an optimist and a pessimist to balance each other out and keep you in the middle. Product-driven financial planners are usually on the optimistic side. They can unconsciously encourage you to invest as much as possible to increase their commission. If you have one of them alone, he or she may make you go beyond your present worth by painting rosy pictures of what will happen if you follow their advice. Certified public accountants are usually more on the realistic and/or pessimistic side. They're fee-driven and generally more conservative. They're useful because they're not as likely to encourage you to take high risks and will rein in your elation. But if you rely solely on them, they could slow you down too much.

You can have the best of both worlds by going to the optimistic financial planner for ideas, then taking those ideas to the pessimistic CPA for feedback. It's a check-and-balance system, and if they both agree, and your experience does, too, then you've probably created a sound team.

Real Estate

Many people think that real estate is a safe alternative for investment, that the stock market is just too volatile and tricky. But the market is only volatile for *people* who are volatile, and you now know how to deal with that. Like anything else, real estate goes through booms and busts. Buying real estate can take up a large proportion of your capital and doesn't always provide the same returns that wise savings and investing can produce. Owning a house doesn't have the same psychological effect as having capital; it carries maintenance and other hidden costs and taxes. Have you ever owned a house but were cash poor, with cash-flow problems? You're emotionally unstable when all your eggs are in one basket like that. Investment rental properties are another alternative, but they can bring their own time-consuming tenant issues.

This isn't to say you shouldn't buy and sell real estate when the property market is favorable, but you don't want to rely solely on it. Even with the availability of equity loans, if you ever really require cash, you may suffer financial setbacks by having to sell during a downturn.

You often hear about people who say, "I made millions of dollars buying a big building downtown," and you might think, *Oh, I've got $10,000 so I should put it into real estate.* The people who made the millions have probably earned the right, through many years of managing their money wisely, to speculate with a small proportion of their wealth. When you try to copy something without having the strategy or understanding to accomplish it, you can receive a big money lesson.

So where does real estate fit into the multistaged savings and investment plan? Your initial home can be purchased right between the first level or cushion account (your money-market reserve account) and the second level (your bonds), but I don't recommend real estate as a sole or initial investment strategy. It requires personal attention and specialized knowledge.

Debt Reduction

Some people focus only on reducing their debts and interest payments. They think they'll start saving "later," when they're finally debt free. Again, having your debt wiped out doesn't have the same psychological incentive as seeing your savings increase. I recommend doing both, even if the debt carries as much as 2 percent more interest than the savings are returning. You'll find a way to pay your debts, but there's no guarantee that you'll train yourself to start saving.

Don't just assume that it's wise to rob your savings to pay off your debts. Most people do that because they value reducing those debts more than they do increasing their savings, and often they find themselves starting all over again with their savings or establishing new debts.

Gambling

What about gambling? Gambling is an attempt at beating the odds or at getting something for nothing. Over time, the "house" is certain to win. I don't advise gambling unless you've earned the right. If you can't handle losing $10,000, don't put it down on the craps table. If you can't handle saying good-bye to $100, don't gamble it. If you have any emotion about losing any sum, you're almost certain to say good-bye to it. You'll know you can handle gambling when you can walk away with absolutely no reaction to either winning or losing.

The financial tolerance level of the average individual is 10 percent; it's a built-in safety net. If you have $1,000, you can handle the loss of $100, but any more and your emotions will kick in. Don't gamble in any way with more than 10 percent of your liquid capital or you'll be almost sure to create reactions in yourself that go far beyond your initial loss.

Know Where You Are

When your finances begin to grow, it's important to keep an eye on them and see what's actually happening. If you focus on your finances, they'll tend to grow. If you invest no energy in them, they'll probably stagnate or die.

You can purchase a software program that easily keeps you abreast of all your finances. I have a money-management program on my computer that lists all my investments: how much I'm investing per month, the yield so far, phone numbers to call in case of difficulties, totals at the end of the month, and so on. It tells me where I am financially, and I can see where I'm growing and at what rate. It takes 20 to 30 minutes at the end of the month to update every page and find out what's going on.

Knowing where you stand financially gives you more certainty and allows you to *act*. Not knowing creates uncertainty and leaves you in a state of *reaction*. Know where you are.

The Consciousness of a Master vs. the Consciousness of the Masses

Human emotions interfere with wealth building more than anything else does. When investors first get into the stock market, if their shares go up they get excited, greedy, and want to buy more. If their shares go down, they get depressed, fearful, and want to sell. That's not a wise long-term strategy; it's a short-term emotional approach, and it's completely opposite financial wisdom.

There's a principle in investing called dollar-cost averaging, and it works like this. Say you buy 100 shares at $1 each, the market takes a dive, and they drop to 50¢. Is that bad? Not if you've done your homework and bought shares in a sound, valuable company. If you spend another $100 at the new price, you'll get 200 shares for the same amount. You then take the average by adding up the total cost and dividing it by the number of shares ($200 divided by 300 shares), and you've brought the price per share down to an average of 67¢. You get more shares of stock per dollar, and when the market inevitably recovers, you *make* more money.

If the price of the stock rises, is that good? Yes and no, because now if you buy more, you're paying a higher price per share. So, contrary to the emotional reaction, you're usually better off holding or buying when shares fall (as long as you have reason to believe they'll eventually rise again), and holding, or in some cases even selling, when they rise.

A couple of years ago, one of my clients' stocks just plummeted. The client was frightened, so I said, "Don't *react*. Don't sell it."

He said, "I have to sell or I'll lose too much. This isn't theory, you know, it's *real money*."

"No, no, no, no, no!" I said. "You're reacting to short-term fear and gratification. Leave it there."

"Okaaay . . . I guess," he said. "But my intuition says . . ."

Again, I replied, "No, that's your emotional fear talking. Don't confuse fear with intuition."

Fear is an instinct that comes from the gut, but intuition comes from the mind and heart. If you listen to your mind and heart, your gut-wrenching fears won't fool you.

Eventually my client calmed down and didn't sell, and the stock went back up within three months.

He called me a few days after it rose and said, "I'm so glad I didn't sell because I would have had a big setback. Thank you for being there to remind me." It helps to have a friend or mentor there when you almost stray from your long-term strategy.

Reacting to daily fluctuations in the market is less wise than following longer-term strategies. The basis of the pyramid structure is that you're a long-term investor. You're in for the long haul, and you simply ride out the temporary emotional oscillations of the mass of investors. You're not a day trader focusing all your energies on the market and trying to make your percentages on lots of little movements. Whether the market goes up or down doesn't mean as much long term. You fall a little here and rise a little there, and the dollar-cost averaging works out to a long, steady rise. History has shown that no matter how far it falls, over time the overall market eventually comes back to a higher level than its previous best. Day to day and month to month, it's volatile, but over years and decades, it still grows.

Opinions are the cheapest commodities on Earth,
and those that circulate the most have the least value.

The masters of investment—the individuals, families, and organizations that have stood the test of time and built fortunes over decades, generations, and centuries—know these principles. The majority of investors don't, and their actions are based not on financial wisdom but on fleeting opinions that change with the weather. There's even an investment philosophy called contrarianism that says to be financially successful all you have to do is the opposite of what the masses are doing. You can hit about 75 percent accuracy that way!

A Wall Street financier once said to me, "If you ever see an investment advertised in every conceivable form, you'd better pull out."

It's common to see investment ads in magazines such as *Worth* and *Forbes,* but if they start showing up in newspapers and glamour magazines, it's time to think twice. Just because the stock or real estate market goes up and people are making money doesn't mean it's time for the fall and big run, the herd phenomenon. When people are leaving their careers in droves to play in the market, making risky margin loan investments and throwing their total savings into too few investments, that's when the market is primed to crash.

Early in 1929, a shoe-shine boy gave multimillionaire Bernard Baruch a hot stock tip. Mr. Baruch went to his office, called his broker, and said, "Sell me out. When shoe-shine boys are giving tips, it's time to get out of the market." That October the biggest crash in financial history struck, but since then the market has risen over and over again to many times its previous record highs. If $100 had been invested into a managed fund in 1928 and left alone, by 2002 it would have grown to $175,178. In contrast, if the same $100 were switched between investments and asset classes as soon as they started to show negative returns, it would have grown to just $86,902 over the 74 years.

Stability and patience are the keys. As a budding financial genius and master, your job is not to listen to the mass consciousness that fears and flees, but to adhere to the tested principles. Don't spring up like a short-lived, flimsy weed. Grow like a great, sturdy oak tree.

Exercise 1

Imagine that your debt payment of $1,000 a month is about to be retired and you're in your last month of payment. If you don't immediately begin saving that same $1,000 a month to replace what you've been paying, your business or income could drop by exactly that amount. Be sure to convert debt payments into savings payments; otherwise, you can finish a payment and mysteriously still break even the next month, even though rationally you'd expect to have that extra $1,000. Unless you dedicate it to your savings, business can mysteriously drop, expenses can mysteriously go up, you can fritter it away, or something can happen to consume that amount.

Having the wisdom to convert your debt to a higher savings purpose maintains your income at the same level but with a different outcome for you. Anytime you're about to finish off a debt payment, start an automatic withdrawal to savings in the same amount the next month. All you're doing is converting debt payments into your own personal wealth; it's merely changing form. Take the debt payment you were giving to other people, and convert it into your own dreams. It's a very powerful action.

Exercise 2

Here's another strange aspect of money metaphysics. Do you have unexpected expenses that come up every month? Car trouble, appliances breaking down or wearing out, a forgotten debt, home repairs, lost cash or possessions? The list is endless. For the average person, these unanticipated expenses add up to between $200 and $600 a month. That's $2,400 to $7,200 a year!

If you want those unexpected and unwelcome expenses to diminish, just work out how much they average for you, and put that exact amount into savings at the start of every month. You think you can't afford them when they come up, but somehow you always do. So go ahead and put that amount into savings . . . and you just *did* afford it. The key is converting disorder into order. When you have enough confidence and trust to invest that much in your spirit, the matter around you breaks down less.

Each person I've put onto this form of forced savings has had fewer unexpected breakdowns in his or her life.

Words of Wisdom and Power

- *I'm wealthy and enlightened; my money comes to me at the speed of light.*

- *When it comes to my finances, I walk before I run and run before I soar.*

- *I stick to my financial strategies no matter what.*

- *I master each financial step as it comes.*

- *I embrace my financial lessons and keep on growing my heavenly wealth.*

- *I have a balanced perspective about building long-term wealth.*

Chapter Eight
The Business
of Business

"The chief business of the American people is business."
— Calvin Coolidge

NOW THAT your savings and investments are under way, it's time to focus on how to accelerate your earnings and business fulfillment to feed them even more. If you have your own business, this chapter will help it take off. If you're presently working for someone else, this chapter still applies to you because you'll probably soon be working for yourself. Those who follow these principles usually end up as self-employed entrepreneurs within three years.

A few of the primary keys to building a great business include having a clear intent or purpose, a truly inspiring vision, a grand message to share, a genuine social calling, and a targeted niche to serve. From these initial basics arise the primary strategic objectives you would love to accomplish or achieve and a plan for their implementation. But before these objectives can be met, the mastery of the mind is to be initiated.

The mental world within you reflects the business world around you. The degree to which you have mastered and organized your own inner life is the degree to which you can master and organize the lives of those around your business. True business leaders are those who are congruent and integrated, and who can organize and lead their inner parts purposefully. *Once leaders govern themselves, they can govern others.*

A principle in business, sometimes called the Peter Principle, states that as you master one level of responsibility, you become promoted to another. Eventually, through promotions, you reach a level of incompetence or a level that's beyond your ability. At that level, you can temporarily or permanently plateau because you won't allow yourself to rise beyond your own level of internal order. Going beyond the plateau requires you to increase your internal order, so first we'll look at how to increase self-mastery and internal order, and then we'll go on to the details of orderly managing and leading others.

Time Is Life

When I was a practicing chiropractor years ago, my slogan was "I align spines and minds with the divine to make people feel fine." I had a large and dynamic practice. One lesson that helped me build such a large practice was realizing that while I was busily adjusting my patients, I wasn't interfering with my employees' work. But when I wasn't adjusting patients, I'd often be in the front office disturbing employees and looking for problems. I noticed that when slow moments arose, I often became distracted by low-priority actions.

It's been said that idle time can be the devil's workshop. When you loaf about, your mind starts thinking about all kinds of doubts, insecurities, fears, other people's beliefs, and worries about what's happening and what isn't happening. Such dead time can become an energy and confidence trap. It can certainly distract your mind. *Any time or space that's not filled with high priorities can automatically become filled with low priorities,* and if you don't *know* your high priorities, you'll fall into the lows.

When I realized this, I made a list of the highest-priority actions I could do during idle moments, so that between patients I could immediately turn to something else of high value. I would write thank-you letters to my patients or memorize their names, their families, their chief complaints, their ages and birthdays, and so on. Every time a patient had a challenging question that I couldn't immediately answer, I'd write it down and make a list of responses, memorize them, and rehearse my response for next time. I'd sit at my desk and read my list of goals and dreams, catch up on professional literature, or work on new slogans and marketing strategies. That's how I came up with the little catch phrase about aligning spines and minds, and it really worked. I had a list of 13 or 14 things to fill my mind during every idle moment. I learned that if I didn't, I'd interfere with my business, distract my time, and worry. If I attended to the list, I just kept *focused.* No matter what happened, I had something worthwhile to do.

Functioning according to higher priorities became such a powerful motivator that I applied it throughout my entire business life. Even when I visited the restroom, I'd take a book and speed-read five pages on the way there, five while standing or sitting, and five on the way back. Four trips a day let me read 60 pages or an extra one to two books per week on whatever I found inspiring or useful. People would ask me, "Why are you so neurotic about this time thing?" and I'd answer, "What you think is neurotic, I believe is efficient." It wasn't neurosis to me. It was the result of the simple observation of what worked and what didn't.

Have you noticed that when you're busy, you often accomplish and create much more? The more intensely you're focused and active, and the longer you maintain such a focus, the faster your accomplishments (time x intensity = results). Time spent on doubt, fear, or low-priority actions slows down your accomplishment process. When you take your mind off your focus, all you see are obstacles. When your mind is focused on your dreams, you don't have *time* for the many self-doubts that block them.

A few years ago, I consulted with a brilliant financial consultant who utilized principles similar to mine. She recorded lists of all her affirmations and dreams, and she clearly defined all the clients she dreamed about working with. She was determined to have some of the wealthiest people in the world as her clients. Wherever she went, she'd carry a tape recorder and headset, and while walking or sitting she'd listen to her affirmations and dreams. People thought she was a bit neurotic, too, but she was more than ten times more financially productive than the other brokers in her firm, and she didn't allow herself much idle time.

Nobody else is offering to make your fulfillment their life focus—it's up to you, so dominate your thoughts on your dreams. I was much more productive than many of my peers because of my discipline and my hierarchy of values. I'd get to the office 30 minutes early, sit down with my eyes closed, and visualize exactly how I desired that day to go. I'd imagine in detail the telephone lines all lit up, people arriving and filling the reception room, myself adjusting them, people coming up and asking, "Dr. Demartini, can I bring in my brother? He really could use your services." I'd concentrate on that scenario, and it's exactly what would happen. I set up a routine with the employees where we'd practice serving imaginary patients. We'd answer invisible telephones, adjust invisible clients, do everything as if we were extremely busy, and the intensity and energy we generated sharpened the team and magnetically drew people to us and built our clinic.

As my business grew, I realized that every moment that wasn't filled with something I loved became filled with something of less importance. Take the time to define your top priorities, because if you don't, your time will be filled with other people's priorities and probably your own fears. Fill your day with high-intensity, high-priority actions. Use every minute, because it's your *life,* and every moment you're not focused on growing high-priority flowers, you're planting weeds. Which will you choose? It's your precious time.

Raise Your Standard

Anything you do consumes time. To maximize the value of your time, prioritize your interactions. People who seem less busy and want to consume your time may think you're being rude when you say no to their invitations, but busy people understand immediately that you're just choosing to prioritize and wisely manage your time.

People who don't value their own time want to take up yours with small talk, and if you keep associating with people who talk small, you could end up with a small life. You'll find out what kind of people they are by putting a fee on your time and raising that fee regularly. If people really value your skills and time, they'll pay for it.

Now, that doesn't mean you have to charge everyone, because some people give you a value and you can see a fair and equitable exchange. Those are the people you want to associate with. They resonate with the next higher vibrational standard. If you continue to grow and your friends don't, there may come a time when you no longer resonate with them and move up to the next group of like-minded souls.

I'm inspired by and have made a personal commitment to growth. That's why I have a little sign on my phone that says: EVERY DAY, I INCREASE MY QUALITY AND STANDARDS. Every day, week, month, and year, strive to increase the quality and standards of your work, and also raise your fee. Otherwise, you'll stay at the level of the weakest link and slowest growth, and you'll deny yourself the inspiration and fulfillment of the next level. That may mean that someday your present associates won't have the money or stamina to keep up with you. Make a commitment to yourself to expand and rise and constantly go to the next concentric level. Your soul is ever calling you to broader and more heavenly financial horizons.

"A man's growth is seen in the successive choirs of his friends."
— Ralph Waldo Emerson

The ability to grow your business requires not only a commitment, but also the willingness to stand up for your worth, and that can be challenging at times.

A gentleman once called my Houston office and said to my managing director, "I'd love to have a lunch meeting with Dr. Demartini here in New York while he's visiting."

She replied, "Fabulous, I'd love to arrange this for you." She arranged the meeting time and pickup place and then continued, "His fee is presently $600 an hour. Will that be by credit card, or will you be bringing a check?"

He said, "Well, I've known John for some time." My director repeated the question concerning my fee, and he finally stated that he would pay at the time with a check. He had me picked up in a town car and driven to his club over Grand Central Station for a fine meal, and for two hours he picked my brain about his business concerns. At the end he said, "I really appreciate this. I have your driver ready downstairs to drive you back."

I said to him, "According to my director, I believe you were to pay for your business consultation by check?"

"Oh, sure, but she said it was $600 an hour, so I told her we were old friends."

"Yes, that's true, but nevertheless, my fee is $1,200."

"You're kidding. Isn't this nice lunch enough?"

I reminded this gentleman that the agreement had been made in advance, and that it was his accountability to pay. I said, "I'm certain that my director was very clear on my fee. Did you somehow assume I would just consult with you for free?"

"I admit I certainly received a great value," he said, "but I thought that since we were old friends, I wouldn't really have to pay."

"I can understand that you may have made that assumption," I replied, "but you're still accountable for paying by check for the services rendered. I believe in fair exchange, and since I was offering you a consulting service and didn't agree in advance to socialize, I am due my fee. I'm only in New York a few days a year, and I may not have chosen to take two hours away from my wife without payment unless I had agreed to socialize in advance."

Although the gentleman was momentarily disturbed, he did pay. Three months later he called once again for my services. This time he had no hesitation about paying, but if I hadn't been clear about my fee the previous time, he might have just assumed that he could invite me for a free lunch again. It's wise to clearly state your fee and stand behind it.

I don't charge everyone who wants to take me to lunch, but this gentleman was attempting to receive a free consultation, so I confronted him. This can sometimes be challenging, but it's wise to keep your wits about you as you grow in self-worth. Be willing to state your fee. If you go below your true heartfelt fee, you'll judge yourself. If you go above it, you'll get elated and eventually be brought back down to what's true. Whenever you try to step outside your true value, you receive a lesson, so decide what your fee is and stick to it.

Efficiency and Effectiveness

Often when you perform a service for less than you feel you deserve, you lower your worth and enthusiasm and slow your business. Even though you may be working like a dog, it's neither efficient nor effective.

I once consulted for a doctor who charged his patients $50 for a three-minute office visit, but only $80 for an initial examination that took 20 minutes. Although new-patient exams were the source of his ongoing business, he wasn't motivated to do them at the lower price. He preferred to do a series of office visits for $1,000 an hour rather than three exams for $240, so he had a subconscious desire not to see new patients and therefore reduced his new-patient business growth. His solutions were to hire someone else to do his exams for less, to charge the equivalent of $1,000 an hour by doing the three exams for more, or to examine faster and charge more.

Any aspect of your work that pays less than you truly feel you deserve can become the weak link of your business. In addition to undermining your motivation, inefficiency and ineffectiveness can also reduce profit margins. When you or your employees do effective actions in an inefficient way, ineffective actions in an efficient way, or ineffective actions in an inefficient way, your business becomes diminished. Your worth can be determined by how efficient and effective you are at performing high-priority actions. Business masters are those who love what they do, do what they love, and work efficiently and effectively. They delegate everything else to those who desire to do the same.

"For where your treasure is, there will your heart be also."
— Matthew 6:21

How can you streamline the actions you take in your business? Ask yourself, "What can I delegate?" Let someone else do the lower-priority tasks that take too much of your time for too little profit. If it's something only you can do, become more efficient at doing it. Otherwise, take the time to train someone else. There may be a time lag before they reach your level of ability, but once they do, you won't concern yourself with it anymore and can get on to your higher priorities. You'll be far more productive, energized, and inspired at the end of the day when you can stick to high-priority actions. *Unless you value your time, neither will the world.*

The following six questions will help you weed out unnecessary activities:

1. **What am I doing that I can stop doing right now? What is superfluous?** You'd be surprised at how much of what you do in a day is just habit, or time filling, because you haven't worked out how to fill your day more productively. Don't be run by routine. When you discover things that aren't necessities, let them go.

2. **What can I redistribute?** Maximize your employees'
    skills by making sure they're all doing what they're
    best at. In a restaurant, you may have someone who's
    excellent at greeting and seating but not so hot at
    remembering orders, so you wisely allocate or special-
    ize them. Someone else might be really fast, so you
    give them a larger section and relieve them of other
    duties. When you allow people to do what they do
    best, they usually give you their best.

3. **Can I standardize and mass produce this?** Years ago,
    I had 1,000 copies of an introductory audiocassette
    tape produced, even though at the time I only needed
    a few. I knew the quality justified using it for some
    time, and I saved myself production costs, time delays,
    and distraction.

4. **What am I doing excessively, and what am I doing
    deficiently?** These two come in matched pairs. You
    may feel that you're paying your employees too much,
    so look for the other side where you may be paying
    too little. You may be underpaying yourself, and you're
    only annoyed because they're seemingly being over-
    compensated when you're not. I find that as long as
    my savings are in place and my investments are grow-
    ing, I'm less concerned about how much my employ-
    ees make. But if they were raking it in and I wasn't, I
    might get a bit reactive and then learn to pay myself
    what I deserve and increase my productivity to com-
    pensate for it.

5. **What am I not confronting?** If you think that you're
    not confronting your employees enough, before
    becoming too aggressive, look for where you might
    already be overly confronting elsewhere. You may be
    yelling at your spouse when you get home, dumping
    your unexpressed assertiveness on your kids, or kicking

the dog and saying, "You don't work a lick and you're getting too many bones, dammit! Get out there and dig more holes!" If you confront and effectively express more at work, you'll moderate your over-confrontation at home.

6. **What products can I produce in the shortest time period to provide the greatest profit?** Once you identify what they are, focus on them.

Your goal is high performance and high priorities. These questions will help you achieve both, receive greater rewards for your efforts, and feel less stressed and more inspired at the end of the day.

Employees

Overall, your employees will probably be less inspired about their work than you'll be about yours. Otherwise, they'd probably have their own company. The few truly inspired beings you find probably won't stay with you long because their own dreams will lead them on. Those who remain and are less inspired can generally be motivated more by pleasure seeking and pain avoidance than by your company's purpose. You'll manage these employees more effectively with equal moments of praise and reprimand. The more skillfully you can balance the two, supporting those who are overly down and challenging those who are overly up, the more effectively you can manage. Your greatest management process, though, will be beyond rewards and punishments—it will be to inspire. The best way to inspire others is for you to become inspired. But you won't remain inspired 24 hours a day, so you'll require checks and balances, penalties and rewards in equal measure. Since you won't want your emotions getting in the way of your business, be sure to hire only those you can equally praise and reprimand or hire and fire.

"If we take people only as they are, then we make them worse; if we treat them as if they were what they should be, then we bring them to where they can be brought."

— Johann Wolfgang von Goethe

Desperation vs. Inspiration

When you hire, don't rescue desperation. Anyone who says, "I'll work for anything, I'll do anything, you can pay me whatever you like" is desperate, and if you hire desperation, you'll breed it in your business.

Before hiring, ask the applicant, "How much do you need to live comfortably, without excessive stress? What's your basic necessity level?" If you have a job paying $3,000 a month, and the applicant says $4,000 a month, you're generally unwise to hire that person unless you have plans to raise the salary quickly. If you do hire the person, you'll be hiring into desperation, and your new employee will bring that desperate energy into your business every day, which can depress the company. You'll probably just be firing them later, after a lot of stress to both of you and cost to your company.

Hire people for purposes of inspiration rather than desperation. I once advertised for a position in my front office and had two applicants. One was a woman with magnificent credentials, but she didn't care about our particular work; and the other wasn't highly qualified, but her whole *dream* was to do the work we were hiring for. One was enthusiastic and the other was stagnant and bored, so I chose inspiration in this case over skills. Many skills you can train, but inspiration isn't easy to develop and actually takes a bit of work. Take the time to evaluate the whole person, not just their curriculum vitae.

To Pay or Not to Pay

Once you hire an employee, remember that you get what you pay for. *If you pay peanuts, you get monkeys.* If you try to pay people *less* than they're worth, they'll feel resentful and depress your business. If you pay them *more* than they're worth, they'll feel guilty about it and distract themselves. It's much wiser and more cost-effective in the long run to pay people what they're truly worth. It keeps them centered and you get a more productive and loyal employee.

If you give your employee a raise, be sure it comes with a corresponding increase in responsibilities. It lowers people's self-worth to get something for nothing, and it's not cost-effective for your business to raise a salary unless you also get a raise in the employee's productivity and value.

I once had a young employee named David who typed research notes for some of my books. He held a moderately skilled position of moderate value, but the longer he was there, the more raises he expected. Finally I explained to him, "Unless we expand your job responsibilities and you consistently produce more, there's no reason to offer you a raise other than to compensate for inflation."

He said, "But I don't want to do more. I enjoy what I do now."

"Then unless you're willing to take on more responsibilities, you won't receive a raise. Just because you've been here for almost a year doesn't guarantee another pay increase. Demonstrate added value to the company and I'll elevate your compensation accordingly. It's not personal, it's business." He then realized that the choice was his. If he wanted to receive more, he was responsible for producing more. Isn't that exactly how a more fulfilling life works?

Busy-ness

A basic principle of nature as well as business is that no organism or organization will intentionally destroy the purpose or reason for its existence, or intentionally cause its own extinction. This also applies to subordinate parts of organizations. If your employees have less than enough work to fill their days, they'll consciously or unconsciously find ways to make sure they still have a job.

I saw this happen with David and his typing. I'd give him a stack of research materials and expect him to type 30 pages a day, but if I was out of town and that stack started to shrink, his productivity would drop. Then I'd return and dump more research materials on him, and he'd magically increase his output. He'd speed up and do 35, 40, even 50 pages a day until he got close to the end of the pile. Then his numbers would fall right off again. He'd slow down to a snail's pace, make errors that required correcting, have machinery mysteriously break down, and find paperwork or mailing to do. If he didn't have enough work, it always seemed that something else would come up to fill his day.

When I gave David more typing to do, he sped up, but when I gave him less typing to do, he tended to slow down—all for the same pay. He'd make sure he never ran out of pages or pay, and that's unconsciously to be expected. When *you* have fewer demands, *you* become more easily distracted and/or anxious. When *your employees* have fewer demands, *they* become less productive. It's up to you to manage them and yourself, to keep your employees busy, focused, and inspired. If you'd love to have your employees be productive, give them just a bit more than they think they can do, and they'll do more than they ever thought possible.

Keep Your Distance

Don't get too close to your employees or clients. If you become too acquainted or intimate with their personal lives, you'll become a less effective manager. When you get too personal with your employees, you diminish your authority. If you get too close to your clients, you diminish your ability to collect from them. Management and collection both rely on authority, and without it both your management effectiveness and collection rate diminish.

Becoming too unprofessional and personal and playing the role of Mr. or Ms. Nice rarely helps you build a big business, but becoming too professional and impersonal and acting like Mr. or Ms. Mean won't build one either. You don't want your employees saying things like, "I haven't met you yet, sir, but I've been working here for 37 years and I'd like to at least look at you from down the hall for a moment."

You want to be able to say yes and no equally—you build respect with your ability to equalize your yeses and nos. If you try to be liked by saying yes all the time, you'll end up minimizing and resenting yourself. Sometime ago, I made up a rule I call the Law of Lesser Pissers, which states that if you're given the choice between pissing someone else off and pissing yourself off, choose *them* every time. Others come and go, but you're with *you* your whole life.

Working on Your Business

Business fulfillment doesn't automatically result from hard work; working smart is just as important. Here are a few important strategies to remember when working on your business.

Raising Fees

Knowing all the details and costs of your business is vital if you're to have clarity and certainty. Knowing where you stand financially tells you how flexible or firm you can be and prevents you from making unwise business decisions. Take the time to work out *all* of your costs and put a true value on yourself and the many portions of your business. It will pay handsomely in the long run, saving you years of undervalued work. By spending just one day examining every cost and profit you have over a year, you'll see where you're doing things of low effectiveness and efficiency, where you're undercharging and overpaying, what your profit margin is, and where the greatest profits are possible. Know your dollar value, or you'll sell yourself short.

How do you raise your fees on your products, services, or ideas? Inform your clients well in advance so they'll be more receptive, and don't raise your fees without offering an increased perceived value. When you're *certain* what your increased value is and you truly feel it's a fair deal, the price-raising process goes much more smoothly. Before raising your fee, make a list of every rebuttal you could possibly receive from your clients, then write and memorize five responses for each one. *Anything you don't have a response for can run and snag you.* If one of the responses doesn't work well, throw it out and come up with another. When the list is ready, print it out and give it to your salespeople.

If you don't have an effective, *memorized* response, your clients may fight you. What do professional athletes or musicians do between games or concerts? They practice. Professional athletes practice between performances, and professional salespeople practice their responses.

Urgency

A few years ago I consulted for a very powerful businessman. He had thousands of employees dispersed over a number of companies. One of his subsidiaries was a diaper-manufacturing company, and his factories also made the clothes for many well-known designers. He was a wealthy and brilliant man. One night over dinner I asked him, "What exactly is the secret to your extraordinary business?"

He said, "The number-one thing to remember is, *everything* is urgent. If you do anything other than the highest priorities, you just won't grow."

He was wise. I've found in my office that if I have a gap between appointments, the patients before and after that gap will take longer and fill it up. Slow or empty time is consumed by low priorities. But if I have my patients booked in tight clusters, my patient flow goes faster and smoother.

If you only have a few clients, appointments, or duties in a day, "cluster book" them—pack them tightly together in the smallest possible time—and watch your energy and effectiveness soar. As you expand the size of the cluster, your business will increase. Act as if you're busy, and watch what happens.

Prosperity and Austerity

Everything occurs in cycles. In times of perceived prosperity, you'll feel elated, optimistic, and complacent, and you'll tend to focus on lower priorities. You'll commonly stop doing the things that brought you there, and the demand for your product or time will drop off while your supply goes up. In times of perceived austerity, you'll feel depressed, pessimistic, and impatient. Then you'll become creative, go back to the basics, and act purposefully once again. As your demand goes back up and your supply goes down, you return to the prosperity side of the cycle. It's a circle, and money dips are an essential part of it until you develop discipline. So embrace the cycle—the ups and downs—but moderate them. When you start to feel prosperous and elated, *that's* the time to get back on focus. When you're at your peak, do what you'd normally do at your bottom. When you're at your bottom, do what you'd normally do at your peak. When you're up, act as if you were down; and when you're down, act as if you were up. Neutralize the swings and keep growing.

Did I?

Ira Hayes was an authority on the laws of success. He was a genius who probably had as much effect on North America as Norman Vincent Peale. Every time he discovered a powerful and effective business idea that truly worked, he wrote it down. He carried the original list with him wherever he went and updated and read it daily.

I learned from Ira and created what I call a "Did I?" form, which is a daily self-mastery checklist. Every time I discovered something that helped my business grow, I added it to the list, and now I review that list at the end of each day.

"Did I?" Form

- ❑ Did I count my blessings and focus on being thankful today?
- ❑ Did I list and prioritize my daily actions today?
- ❑ Did I act on my priority actions today?
- ❑ Did I communicate in terms of people's values today?
- ❑ Did I share from my heart while speaking today?
- ❑ Did I write at least one thank-you letter today?
- ❑ Did I grow and accelerate my wealth today?

I've already proven to myself that each item on the list is effective and important, so if I miss any, I make a note and leave it on my desk. The next morning, I review it and commit to focusing on any areas I'm not maintaining. The "Did I?" form has become more than just a checklist. It's my daily personal manager and an incredibly useful tool.

Feedback

Make sure you request feedback about your products and services. Why? To keep refining and evolving what you do and how you do it. Not every suggestion will be of the greatest value, but by being selective, you can receive tremendous feedback.

Unsolicited advice isn't always valuable, especially since those who *do* are constantly receiving unsolicited advice from those who *don't*. People occasionally tell me, "You ought to do this and you ought to do that," but when I ask them, "So, are you doing seminars around the world?" they step back and say, "Oh no, of course not." That doesn't mean they don't occasionally have sound ideas, but as a rule, if you're not willing to pay for their advice, you're probably not going to pay attention to it. It's wiser to receive counsel from those who've been there and have achieved success.

Work and Play

During your business career, you'll experience moments of work and play, seriousness and humor, and tragedy and comedy. If you're wise, you'll embrace them all equally, for each pair will help you remain centered and focused. If you make your business too serious, either some employee will try to create fun to provide the balance, or you'll feel urges to take time off and get away to express the playful side of your nature. Put work and play together and you and your employees will be more integrated, energetic, and inspired. The purpose of life is *life,* and it requires two sides to be complete.

Put Your Heart in It

When you truly appreciate and value where you are and what products or services you have to offer, so will others. Whatever you think about and focus on with inspiration is what you attract into your life. Clear away anything that's in the way of your heavenly inspiration. How can an appreciative and inspired life do anything but bring you more wealth and closer to heaven? It's a basic law of business. Until your innermost dominant thought is your clients, don't expect their innermost dominant thought to be your business. When *they* are on *your* mind, *you* are on *their* mind.

The Formula for Business Explosion

- Know your business purpose and objectives.

- Organize your financial house.

- Focus on high priorities.

- Fill your mind with what you'd love and allow no idle time.

- Know your costs, set your fees, and stick to them.

- Continually raise your standards and fees.

- Organize your place of business so it's clean, efficient, and beautiful.

- Throw away anything that doesn't serve your priorities, and throw away anything you wear that doesn't make you feel like a multimillionaire.

- Put your heart into your business.

- Treat your business with love.

Exercise 1

I once addressed 1,000 employees and asked, "How many of you would love to know more about where you stand in the eyes of your supervisor or employer?" All the hands went up.

One of your employees' greatest frustrations may be not knowing where they stand. People become more focused and present when you guide them with a balance of positive and negative feedback. When you both know what their strengths and weaknesses are, you can discuss how to apply or capitalize upon them.

The following employee evaluation is a gem. It lets employees know exactly where they stand and assures increased productivity.

Write down a list of all the character traits you expect from your employees, and make them known. Then every quarter, you (or whoever manages the employee) can sit down with each employee and go through the list. Both you and the employee give your evaluation of the employee's performance, with the employee going first. Use the numerical rating system 1 = poor, 2 = fair, 3 = good, 4 = superior.

With 38 traits on my list, this was the scoring system (out of a possible 152):

Below 74	Unsatisfactory; dismissal
74 to 85	Probation; merit raise zero percent
86 to 101	Below average; merit raise 2 percent
102 to 117	Average; merit raise 4 percent
118 to 136	Above average; merit raise 8 percent
Above 136	Outstanding; merit raise 10 percent

Do this evaluation every quarter and your employees will be more motivated and self-managing. When raises come up, you'll both know whether or not they deserve one, and why.

Exercise 2

Running a business requires capital and sometimes entails degrees of debt. Apply the following rules of debt:

1. Be grateful for your lenders. They represent someone who believed and invested in you or your business.

2. Reduce your total debt payments down to an hourly amount.

3. Convert debt into client service.

Imagine you owe $100,000 to a bank and your payments are approximately $2,100 a month for five years. Your normal response may be to think, *Oh no, I'm $100,000 in debt!* But, imagine that you generate $1,000 a day (if you don't yet, you soon could), and you see ten clients or do ten business transactions a day. That's $100 per client. If you work 20 days a month and have a 50 percent overhead, that means you only need to see 2.1 clients per day to make your loan payment. When you look at debt that way, it's not so overwhelming, is it?

Whatever your debts, total them up and translate them into service. Instead of thinking of the debt, focus on the service you can provide. When you focus on and worry about your debts, your state of mind repels opportunities and business and your clients drop. But if you focus on serving your clients, your debt drops. Don't focus on what you want to see die (debt), focus on what you want to see live (client growth). Convert whatever you feel burdens you into that which inspires you. *Focus on what inspires your life, and watch your heavenly profits and wealth grow.*

Words of Wisdom and Power

- *Every day, I raise my standards and quality.*

- *I fill my life with high priority and intensity and receive the rewards.*

- *I receive nothing less than what I am worth.*

- *I plant so many inspiring business flowers that there is no room for weeds.*

- *I am a professional, and I practice between my performances.*

- *When my clients are on my mind, I am on their mind.*

Chapter Nine
Marketing Magic

"Nothing happens in this world until somebody sells something to somebody."

— Walter Hailey

EVERYONE IS in marketing and sales, whether they know it or not. Beauty, strength, intelligence, kindness, wealth, power— they're all ways to advertise your value as a human being, and they attract other humans to you. Even plants are engaged in marketing when they put out flowers. Their colors and perfumes draw insect customers to their products (the nectar and pollen). A fair exchange of labor and reward takes place, life blossoms, and beauty is the vehicle of the transaction. That's how life *works.*

If you believe that sales and marketing are not respectable or somehow manipulative, you're setting yourself up against the forces of nature. You'd be wise to have a change of heart because sales and marketing are a part of the divine order and are vital ingredients in your fulfillment.

There are four magical feelings that put energy and sizzle into your life: gratitude, love, inspiration, and enthusiasm. It's the *sizzle* that makes the difference. When Mexican restaurants discovered that when they made a display of carrying sizzling fajitas to the table, they sold more fajitas. If you go into the marketplace and you don't sizzle, why would people buy from you? It's wise to be creative, dance with the market, play with the selling, and put some enthusiasm into your work. The more vitality and energy you put into whatever you do, the greater the results.

Enthusiasm comes from the
Greek words en *(within) and* theos *(god).*
It means, literally, the god within.

Years ago, a well-respected professional speaker and business leader gave me some advice on marketing. He said, "You won't be concerned about selling your next seminar if you give everything you have to the seminar you're presenting. Become totally present and inspired, and the next one will take care of itself." The best marketing step you could ever take is to be present and inspired with whatever you're doing and whomever you're with. Enthusiastic energy is pure spirit, and spirit is the most radiant and magnetic of all forces. When you love yourself and become inspired, so will others. Marketing is a test of how much inspiration, self-love, and other-love you have, as well as your ability and certainty in communicating it.

Sell Yourself

In the pursuit of profit and heavenly wealth, any portion of your mental faculties that remains undeveloped can become your stumbling block. If you become uncertain, if you won't honor yourself enough to speak an inspiring one-minute commercial about your value to the world and what you have to offer, why would the world want to buy from you? *Nobody else gets up in the morning to sell you; the only person on Earth with that responsibility is you.* If you don't learn to do it skillfully and wholeheartedly, you won't masterfully direct your destiny. When you can confidently sell yourself to yourself, you'll confidently sell yourself to others.

To create that level of certainty, take a moment to do the following:

1. Write down your *services.*

2. List the *features* that make them unique.

3. Describe how they are of *utility* to the public.

4. List the *advantages* of your work or services over anybody else's.

5. Describe the specific *benefits* you offer and what *value* your services fill in the world.

Keep answering these questions over and over again until you feel a deep sense of increased worth, certainty, and appreciation for the service you provide. You're the hardest sell you'll probably ever face, and when you're certain of the value of your skills or product, everyone else will be easy to sell. Unless you value yourself, don't expect anybody else to. Until you've sold yourself, don't expect anybody else to buy.

When you're convinced, the next step is to convince others, so sit down and ask yourself this question: *What are all the possible rejections I might meet in selling myself or my product?* Then make a list of five responses for each one until you have absolute certainty that you can face any situation with confidence.

When somebody says, "I'm not *interested;* please don't bother me," if you don't have a reply ready you'll take it personally and possibly beat yourself up. But if you're prepared, you can say, "Fabulous! That's just the reaction I was hoping for! About 94 percent of the people who buy my product say just that initially. This is wonderful!" Prepare a response that allows you to play with the situation and you won't fall into self-doubt or judgment. Say,

"I was actually just calling you to practice. Thank you for the chance to work on rejection," and instead of facing a closed door, you open communication with humor. Anything you *don't* have a response for runs you, but anything you *do* have a response for turns into an opportunity. Selling is a dance, and when you know the steps, it's an enriching and inspiring experience.

"Take your work seriously, but take yourself lightly."

— Ron Lee, the Corporate Ninja

Sell the Seller

Nothing ever gets done until someone sells something to someone else, be it a product, service, idea, or vision. Whoever has the most certainty makes the sale. Distributors used to come into my office regularly, and my first reaction was, "What a hassle. These people are interfering with my business, and I don't want to deal with them." Eventually I saw them for what they really were— *opportunities*. When they came to make the sale, I made the sale.

We had a great routine. People selling telephones, insurance, stationery, or whatever would walk in, glance at my business card to get my name, and say, "Good morning, I'd like to speak to Dr. Demetriano. He's a personal friend of mine." My front desk receptionist would smile and give them a new-patient form, saying, "You'd like to speak with the doctor? Fine, please fill out this form and he'll be with you in just a few minutes." Some would automatically fill it out, not knowing why they were filling out a case-history form about their health. Others would say, "No, no, I think there's been a mix-up. There's nothing wrong with me, I just want to talk to him for . . . personal reasons."

"That's fine, but Dr. Demartini has given strict instructions that he doesn't speak or do business with anyone unless they're a patient."

"Oh, why is that?"

"He wants to make sure they're shooting straight from the hip, that they're level-headed and not crooked. He's a chiropractor, you know. It's the balance thing."

Some of them would laugh and say, "Tell you what, I'll come back when he's not so busy," and we wouldn't have to deal with them. But if they stayed for an exam, I'd let them make their pitch. That gave *me* time to influence them with my certainty about my work and its value to them, and roughly one in four solicitors actually became patients. The purpose of marketing and advertising is to bring people to you, so if they come of their own accord, that's free marketing. Instead of it being an annoyance, be prepared and turn it into an opportunity by asking the question "How do I make the sale when they come to make the sale?"

Am I a salesperson? You bet. Be proud to be a salesperson; that's what makes the world go 'round. Say to yourself, "I'm a master salesperson, and when they come to make the sale, I make the sale. I know all the objections, I know what to say, and my magnetism and my product sell themselves. I *love* being a salesperson." Loving what you do and doing what you love is one of the secrets of fulfillment and heavenly profits.

Be Outrageous

The masterful marketer is the one who's willing to do what most people wouldn't even consider. When I was 22, I took a job selling suits in a department store at a local mall, with a tiny base salary that a goldfish would have struggled to live on. I thought I could supplement it with my sales commission, but I didn't know that the store had few customers. After two weeks of pacing around the men's section, becoming bored and earning little, I realized that it was time to get creative. It seemed to be a choice between quitting and poverty. So of the four choices—quitting, poverty, both, or neither—I chose neither and made up my own option. I decided that if customers weren't going to come to me, I'd better go to them.

I went into the back supply room and found a long clothing rack with wheels. I loaded it up with dozens of suits, shirts, and ties, and I set off in search of customers. I strolled up and down that mall wearing one of the suits as advertising and dragging the others. I wandered out onto the front sidewalk and nearly down to the street. I even went in front of the other stores to make sales. I approached everyone. I sold suits to businessmen and to ladies for their husbands at home. I would have sold suits to dogs if they'd had any money. I laughed and joked, offered little imaginary prizes, had strangers try suits on for other people to admire, and made real fun out of it. *Nobody* had acted like me before, and people were either charmed or alarmed, but my sales went through the roof. My commissions grew larger than the store manager's! As a result, and because of his insecurities and envy, he changed the storewide commission structures. Of course, once that occurred, there was little incentive left for me to stay. But I was grateful for the opportunity because I'd discovered a real knack for selling, and saw how to go beyond my comfort zone and take risks.

Learning about the art of selling helped me immensely as the years rolled by. When I moved from my first office to my beautiful new second office on the 52nd floor of a magnificent skyscraper in uptown Houston, I was once again able to apply what I'd learned about selling. When I sold my first practice, I also relinquished many of my existing patients because I wanted to raise my fees, conduct a cash practice, and concentrate on the city's elite. So there I was, sitting in my expensive new office with *no* patients and saying, "Hmmm."

Knowing that the more people I meet and greet, the more I treat, I thought, *I guess it's time to go out and meet new people.* So I headed for the lobby to begin meeting people. As I rode the elevator down, I noticed that nobody was talking. It was dead silent, and I got this idea: *Perfect! Elevator seminars!* When the elevator reached the lobby, I held the doors open. Wearing an official-looking blue suit, I waited until the elevator was filled with 20 people. I packed 'em in like sardines and got on last, and when the doors closed, I spun around like Michael Jackson. I'd timed the trip and knew I had 28 seconds to make my sales pitch.

I said, "Hi! I'm Dr. Demartini. Welcome to my spinal education class. Please repeat after me: Bone out, irritate nerve, cause problem—subluxation. Bone in, relieve nerve, cause life—adjustment. The power that made the body heals the body from above down, inside out. I'm Dr. Demartini, and I align spines and minds with the divine, to make people feel fine. I practice galactic chiropractic, and only accept space cases." As the door opened, I passed out my cards. People left that elevator absolutely stunned, asking each other, *"What was that?"*

The instant everyone exited, I hit the button, descended once again, picked up another 20 people, and kept going. The more I did it, the easier and funnier it became. There were 4,000 people working in that building, and I met most of them that way. I signed up 40 new patients that first month. A great number of people wanted to go to this crazy chiropractor during their breaks. The author of a book called *Power Networking* happened to be on the elevator one day and described his experience in one of his chapters on building businesses. He wrote, "Man, that guy was gregarious as *hell*." To this day, there are still people in Houston who refuse to ride the elevator with me, just in case I decide to do a little marketing.

To be a great salesperson, you'd better be willing to do the action steps that most people aren't willing to do. It's all in how you view it, how much energy and certainty you have, and how creative you can be. If you'd love to rise above the common crowd, then stand above them—sales mastery demands it.

"When one door closes another door opens; but we often look so long and so regretfully upon the closed doors that we do not see the ones which are open for us."
— Alexander Graham Bell

To Sell Is Not to Tell

There are two primary types of marketing: centrifugal and centripetal. Like centrifugal force, in which objects are impelled outward from the center, centrifugal marketing means taking a new idea and selling it to the world, whether people are looking for it yet or not. Centripetal force utilizes the opposite effect—moving objects inward toward the center—and centripetal marketing means finding out what people are already looking for and providing it. Both types of marketing have their place and value.

Robert Schuller, the world-renowned spiritual teacher and minister, was certainly a master of centripetal marketing. After graduating from divinity school and serving briefly at a church in Illinois, he was invited to start a new church in California. When Schuller and his wife arrived, they had $500, no building, and no congregation. He went door to door, asking people where they went to church, what denomination they belonged to, and what they wanted in a church. He discovered that they didn't want to get all dressed up, then fight with the kids to get them clean and ready. They didn't mind going to church, but they wanted to come as they were, have the experience quickly, and get back home so they didn't lose too much of their weekend.

What did Schuller do with this information? He made a list of places that weren't being used on Sunday mornings, such as school auditoriums, warehouses, and other ministries that held their services on Saturdays. Ultimately, he approached a drive-in movie theater with 500 parking spots and individual speakers on stands and asked if he could rent it for his church. On Sunday mornings it was vacant anyway, so they gave it to him for minimal costs. He built a pulpit on the roof of the snack bar, connected a microphone to the speaker system, and put a little sign on the road. He then went door to door again, telling people where he was holding services.

It was brilliant marketing, and people came in droves. They'd drive in, park their cars, and listen to the service through the little speakers that attached to their car windows. Schuller was so effective that soon he was able to build his own church. What began as a door-to-door investigation of people's needs turned into the Crystal Cathedral, the beautiful glass church where he preaches to thousands of people every Sunday morning. And he still has an "in-car worship" option alongside the cathedral, on the site of the original drive-in church.

Centrifugal marketing is when you have a dream or inspiration that you'd love to share whether people are looking for it or not, and you motivate and inspire them to become interested in it. Robert Schuller had a dream he wanted to share, but he cleverly also used centripetal techniques to tailor it to the needs of the public. If you master centripetal marketing, you receive input from many buyers. If you master centrifugal marketing, you broadcast output from one seller. Ideally, you want to combine both—have a dream that inspires you and learn how to communicate it in an effective manner that inspires others. Ask, "How can I provide others what they would love by providing myself with what I would love, and how can I provide myself what I would love by providing them what they would love?"

To Sell Is to Ask

The wisest way to build your business is for both you and your customer to have your values fulfilled. Have an inspiring product or service you would love to bring to people, and then polish it up according to their feedback. The aim of marketing is to truly understand and love your customers so well that your product or service fits them like a glove and sells itself. To sell is not to tell; to sell is to ask, and keep on asking until you know exactly what your customers are looking for. Then present your product in terms of their values or needs and the sale is almost automatic.

One of my dreams is to help awaken people around the world to how much love and wisdom they already have within them. But if I were to just blurt my message out upon meeting someone, I'd probably be ineffective.

If I said, "Come to my seminar and you'll discover how much love and wisdom you have within," they could easily respond,

"But I don't *want* more love in my life. I just split with my wife, and she's *suing* me."

If I approached people in this manner, they'd disappear in a flash. Although the benefit I could offer them is real, I haven't expressed it in terms of their values at the time.

Instead, what if I asked a series of questions that unveiled people's needs and values, where they in turn revealed to me how I could market and ultimately sell to them? What if I first helped them clarify their problem or void, or what appears missing, and then offered a solution? If you don't know your customers' dominant buying motive, you'll be banging your head against a wall trying to sell to them.

The Seven Stages of Selling

There are seven basic stages to selling. Be sure to follow the stages in order. If you skip a stage, life will find a way to remind you to go back to that stage until it's complete. Each stage is accomplished through asking a series of questions. Remember, to sell is not to tell; to sell is to ask.

1. **Greet or introduce.** *Hi, my name is John Demartini. What's your name?* Make sure you introduce yourself with a smile. People form opinions within the first three to five seconds of meeting you, so your voice, dress, eye contact, and manner are crucial here.

2. **Establish rapport.** Similarities forge bonds. The quicker you can ask people questions about their lives that lead to common threads between you and them, the easier it is to sell.

3. **Identify their need.** What's their primary or immediate need? Find out what appears to be missing or problematic in their lives. The numbers of rejections you receive during the selling process are inversely proportional to

how well you've established their need or void. The deeper and broader their need, the easier it is to sell.

4. **Confirm their need.** Be certain that you've established their true need. When they've told you what their need or void is, repeat this back to them. It's wiser to know than to assume or guess.

5. **Offer value.** Tailor your work as a solution to their issue. Make an offer they can't refuse. If someone says they can't afford or don't want something, all that means is you haven't demonstrated value in their terms—so communicate more value! People never have a lack of money, they have a lack of motivation. If you provide the motivation, they'll find the money.

6. **Close.** Make the sale. Don't leave it vague—confirm the appointment, get the credit-card details, and arrange delivery and payment. Make it happen.

7. **Provide service.** Deliver the service you promised.

The art of selling requires the ability to listen, so listen carefully and tailor your questions to fit your potential customers' responses and needs. *Link your services or products to your customers' specific values and your products will sell themselves.* It's all in the way you ask questions and communicate your value. Be sincere and genuinely interested. Honestly care. Be sure that your product or service truly fits their needs and values. If you try to fool people, they'll eventually catch on. When you're sincere and speak from your heart, they'll respond most favorably.

Sometimes you may need to vary this seven-stage theme. There are times when the most effective sales technique is to say less. Sometimes during the first couple of stages, I may just give very short answers if and when people ask me what I do. Then I turn the conversation back to them, and they become increasingly interested about my life and my work. When they're sufficiently intrigued, they'll provide me with enough information so I can address their values more succinctly. Remember, to sell is not to tell. To sell is to ask. And occasionally it's best to just be silent. Silence has power.

Added Value

Find a way to provide people that little extra something. It makes all the difference.

Let me give you an example. I turned my office into a *major* place for people to network. I'd memorize my clients' personal and business details, and when I met someone whose needs matched a client's business, I'd bring them together. I'd take the time to go out to the front counter and say to my receptionist, "I'd love for you to schedule Mr. Davis for 3:00 tomorrow when Ms. Fitch is coming in. His company needs a new logo and letterheads, and she owns a design firm." By coming to me, they actually increased their business and would refer more people to me because I was referring people to them. It's called added value. Showing an extra interest in them secured their return to my business. So ask yourself, "What added value can I offer my clients today? What will make them feel extra special and make our company special, too?"

Testimonials

There's a great value in having your satisfied clients speak for you. It's independent marketing of your skills to other clients, but it's even more important for you and your employees. I've consulted for companies in trouble and asked, "Have you been requesting and receiving testimonials from your clients?"

Usually they say, "Uh, not recently."

"Well, every time you have a satisfied or grateful client, ask them to write you a testimonial concerning your services. Receiving acknowledgment for your service and for the difference you make in your clients' lives is essential." I've seen companies begin growing again in a matter of weeks just because they started receiving feedback in the form of testimonials. If you don't feel worthwhile, you lose heart; when you know you're of value, you reopen your heart.

Praise and Blame

On the road to achievement and fulfillment, perceptions of success and failure or praise and criticism are inevitable. Criticism and praise will maintain equilibrium throughout your life no matter what you do, and your only choice is the form they take. If you aren't willing to step out and face criticism from the outside, you'll do it internally. You'll criticize the hell out of yourself, because nobody escapes criticism. But the instant you're willing to embrace it from the outside, it diminishes within you. In other words, if you allow *others* to criticize you, *you* won't have to do it. The master in any field is willing to pay the price of mastery, and part of that price is the ridicule and condemnation that come from stepping outside the boundaries that limit most people. *Honor and criticism come together as a pair,* so if you're not willing to experience more blame, you won't be able to receive more praise. If you fear failure, success will elude you.

A well-known professional speaker once told me how he learned to deal with audiences who didn't easily laugh. He said, "I learned to laugh at myself. Once I could do that, it didn't matter if my jokes bombed because I got to laugh. And then because *I* laughed, people laughed at *me,* so I got a laugh anyway." We beat ourselves up with the false idea that we should be successful in everything we do, but he learned to play with it.

A troubled man went to his wise and good old rabbi and said, "Rabbi, I am a failure. More than half the time I do not succeed in my life. Please tell me something wise."

"My son, I give you this wisdom. Look on page 930 of the 1970
New York Times Almanac, and you may find peace of mind."
It was a listing of the lifetime batting averages of the greatest
baseball players, and Ty Cobb, the greatest of them all,
had a .367. Even Babe Ruth couldn't touch him.

The man went back to his rabbi and said,
"Ty Cobb, .367, that's it?"

And the rabbi replied, "Right. Ty Cobb, .367.
He got a hit one time in three.
He didn't even bat .500, so what can you expect?"

"Ah!"

— Robert Fulghum

Paradigms

When I published a new book some years ago, I was told that the average author sells 10,000 copies, and the publishers take a small profit, stop printing, and go on to the next book. It's called fodder, and I was told that there was little I could do about it. But I said, "Hell, my vision is a lot bigger than that. I will *personally* buy 10,000 copies and sell them myself."

You'd be surprised at how many people blindly accept beliefs and outcomes. I invested the time and energy, and that book took off. I asked my publishers at the time, "How many TV and radio interviews do you have in mind for the launch?" and they said, "Oh, we could probably get as many as *ten* and that would be great." That was the limit of their vision, but I did 25 TV shows on satellite to 25 cities in *one day.* It took four hours in one studio—every ten minutes I did another interview.

Beware of paradigms and limiting belief systems, because they're usually not true. People told me that the average doctor is highly challenged for six months after graduation, but I received *five times* the number of patients they projected. That was the paradigm, though, and many of the students who graduated lived that limit. *The impossible is simply another business opportunity* means there's a niche that's free and available. No one will compete with you because they think it's impossible! Start your own paradigm. The cost may be working with greater intensity than most people would or even could do, but when you decide to do whatever it takes, travel whatever distance, and pay whatever price, you'll reap the results. How inspired and committed are you?

Chunk It Down

My dad used to say to me, "Find out what it costs you to acquire a new customer, to service a customer, and what margin you make from a customer. Then you'll know what your income requirements are every day, and you'll be less anxious about your future."

One of the most powerful real estate developers in the world lives in New York. He looked at his meeting rate per new client and worked out how many people he had to meet each day to sell a certain amount of property. His ambition became not only to sell property, but also to get face-to-face with the decision makers. He knew that if he connected with a certain number of decision makers on real estate every day, he'd probably meet his target, so he saw only those who could qualify for the sale, and he wouldn't finish the day until he'd made his numbers. His whole focus was on being in the right place at the right time and meeting the right people, and he became one of the most powerful developers in the world. So chunk your objective down, and focus on the most probable and highest-quality prospects.

I'm always in the right place at the right time
to meet the right people to make the right deal.

Increasing and Diminishing Utility

When you first hear a song on the radio, you may think it's just okay. The second time you hear it, you really like it. The third time, you think it sounds great. You want to hear it again and again, you tell other people, and you look forward to hearing it. Or you find a new restaurant, go back the next day, and for three months you and your friends eat there almost every day. When something is new and exciting, it temporarily increases in value; this is the Law of Increasing Utility. But one day you know every note of that song, or you've been through the menu twice and know how all the food tastes. When something is old and becoming boring, it decreases in value; then it follows the Law of Diminishing Utility. Every product, service, or idea has a cycle of increasing and decreasing utility.

There are fads, trends, and classics. When you offer a fad, like the pet-rock fad 25 years ago, the Law of Diminishing Utility applies much sooner and you'll be required to sell quickly to a lot of people. If you reach the peak of increasing utility and you don't have the next product or service in place, the Law of Diminishing Utility will automatically take your profits down. You must continually come up with new ideas, services, products, and value.

The 80/20 Law

Also known as the Pareto Principle or Joseph Juran's Rule, the 80/20 Law states that 20 percent of what you do gives you 80 percent of your results, and 80 percent of what you do gives you 20 percent of your results. It's the same with clients, so focus most on that top 20 percent and put your greatest attention and effort into your key customers or clients.

People approach me at seminars and ask, "Can you send me some information on your seminars, books, and tapes?"

I ask them, "What specific information would you love to receive?" If they can't be specific about what they're interested in, I often decide not to send them information. If they desire a specific product, I'll gladly fill out the form and make the sale right there. But I know statistically that many of those unspecified mail-outs yield little returns. It's a poor expenditure of time, energy, and money.

Give your greatest attention to your most inspiring clients, because even though they're much fewer in number, they return many times more profit. Don't concentrate on cold clients at the expense of warm ones. It's simple physics.

Gestalt

Neurolinguistic programming, or NLP, is a method for analyzing and accessing consciousness. Popularized by Richard Bandler and John Grinder, NLP deals with how people communicate. It classifies people in terms of three main divisions of attention and information uptake—visual, auditory, and kinesthetic or feeling—and describes how to most effectively approach each type. For example, if you use a lot of gestures, the "visual" person will love it. The "auditory" person may relate best if you use words and phrases related to hearing, such as "How does that sound to you? Does this ring a bell?" If they're "kinesthetic" or feeling, they'll respond best if you can get them up to dance or interact in some hands-on way.

NLP is true up to a point—individuals are inclined toward one of the three categories—but it only applies to their outer persona or mask, not their true inner being. Their dominant persona has a dominant accessing system, but there's really no such thing as a visually, auditorially, or kinesthetically dominated *being*. A person's true nature or inner soul is a gestalt, an integrated and synthesized whole. If you try to use visual, auditory, or kinesthetic techniques to communicate with your clients, you're only talking to their persona, not who they truly are.

When you're inspired, all three types come out together. At that moment, you transcend any sensory category. Inspiration integrates all of your personas and you spontaneously attune equally with all three of another person's at once. When you're certain and inspired about what you do, effective and congruent methods become automatic. Speak from a state of gestalt and the details will take care of themselves. When you speak from your heart, your heart will touch other hearts. In that state, extraordinary and heavenly business outcomes happen.

I once presented a program from 2:00 P.M. until 9:00 P.M. because I became so present that everyone lost track of time and space. We didn't stop for dinner or a restroom break, and no one even noticed. Because I remained in an inspired state for seven hours, because I went into my heart and spoke to their hearts, there was no separation between the audience and me. That's the true gestalt, the real sizzle, the integration, and it has tremendous power to move and impact people. That was when I was truly present and when there was gratitude, love, enthusiasm, and inspiration in the room. No one who was there has forgotten it.

True inner marketing goes beyond general outer marketing. It's a state of your most radiant being that transforms everyone it touches—it's your *spirit*. Surprisingly, even advertising and marketing can take you to heaven. Do what you love and love what you do, and one day you'll find yourself spontaneously doing everything described in this chapter and in this book.

Exercise 1

This exercise is called the Embodiment Exercise. Write down your top ten clients, in order of priority. Then take the top two and write down the ten character traits they display most. What is it about them that makes them such great customers?

Incorporate those ten qualities into your business. To attract a certain quality of client, be willing to live out the character traits you admire in them. If you'd love your clients to be punctual, be punctual. If you'd love them to pay in advance, do it first. If you want them to refer others, tell people about the businesses you patronize. Integrity, referrals, gratitude—whatever you desire in a client, do it yourself and watch what happens.

This will help you put your own business in order, and it's an extremely powerful technique for attracting ideal clients through the principle of resonance.

Exercise 2

At the end of each business day, list the names of all the clients you personally did business with, and write each of them a brief thank-you letter. Thank them for trusting you enough to come to you. Thank them for the time and money they dedicated to you. Thank them for their appreciation and courtesy. Thank them for the opportunity to do what you love and get paid for it. Whatever you're grateful for, write it down.

You needn't send the letter unless you'd love to. The purpose is to focus your mind on your work and clients with gratitude. Whatever you're grateful for increases. *Whatever you think about and thank about, you bring about.*

Words of Wisdom and Power

- *I'm a master salesperson. My magnetism and products sell themselves.*

- *When they come to make the sale, I make the sale.*

- *I do what other people are unwilling to do.*

- *To sell is not to sell; to sell is to ask.*

- *How can I provide others what they would love so I can provide for myself what I would love?*

- *I am a master at identifying voids and offering values.*

- *I embody all the qualities of my greatest clients.*

- *The impossible is simply another business opportunity.*

Chapter Ten
The Myth of Retirement

"People don't get old. When they stop growing, they become old."

— Anonymous

THERE'S A pervasive and limiting illusion concerning time and aging, and unconsciously buying into it can diminish both your life and your fortune, while seeing through it can add years to your life and wealth to your worth. Many people believe that youth is a heavenly time of optimism and energy before the "hellish" decline into old age and death. That's true only if you make it so, and you really do have the power to choose. This pernicious myth has little to do with the reality of life and human potential. Chronological age is certainly not the only determining factor.

There is inside you, from a time before you ever became aware of it, a vision and calling to do something extraordinary. The age of your body can't touch this divine soul or spark that calls you to shine. However the candle of the body may waver, this light of spirit never goes out. You're not made in anything but an image of greatness, and deep down inside you have something remarkable that you'd love to share, accomplish, and be. Everyone has this spark, and there's no end to it because it's beyond who you think you are. It's a fragment of divinity that doesn't age or die, and it's your true nature. It doesn't matter if you're 20, 50, or 80 years old, you have an immortal purpose and a dream that seeks fulfillment.

As I mentioned earlier, I was only 17 when I met a 93-year-old man who gave me such inspiration and vision that he changed the direction of my life. He played a major role in making me who I am today. His vision was so clear that he didn't question it, and he communicated that certainty to just about everyone he touched. It's impossible to meet someone with an unwavering purpose without being inspired and guided by them, just as a plant can't help but respond to the life, warmth, and direction provided by the sun. His wisdom was a result of his age, experience, and vision, and he utterly transformed my ideas about what aging can be. Since then, I can't count the number of highly motivated, vibrant individuals I've been blessed to meet who also happened to be well past the prescribed age of "retirement."

This chapter consists of stories that illustrate the unending aspiration of the soul to be of use to the world. In each of them, people were faced with the myth of retirement and discovered the truth that they were made for something greater. Their experiences apply to you and to me and to everyone, because in this way we're all alike. You don't run out of time, you only shut out your inspiration. If you're nearing retirement, your timing in reading this is perfect. If you're not, this may be your opportunity to transcend a myth in advance and change the way you think about, and manifest, your future.

I'm in Business

I was giving my Breakthrough Experience program in Dallas a few years ago, and one gentleman there was in his 72nd year

He'd been retired for seven years, not doing much of anything at all with his days, and a friend had suggested he might benefit from attending this two-day event. For most of the first day, he really wasn't connecting to what was going on. I wasn't able to reach him, and I could tell he had a belief in his mind that said, *Well, this is fine for young people, all this mission and achievement and destiny stuff, but not for someone my age. It's too late for me.*

I sat with him as he was completing the core event of the weekend, the Quantum Collapse Process. I knew his heart wasn't in it, so I had him pause in his work and asked, "Do you honestly believe there's nothing left for you to do on this planet?"

He said, "Why do you say that?"

"Because I look at your energy and your spirit," I said. "You're not really participating or present with much around you. It's like . . . it's like you're dying."

"Is it that obvious?" he asked.

"Yes, that's what I see, a man who's dying because he's lost his dream, his vision, his inspiration and purpose." I find that when you speak from your heart, people know it, and they'll let you go far beyond the normal limits of "acceptable" behavior.

His eyes misted up a little and he said, "I had no idea anyone could see it, but that's exactly how I feel. Now I know why my friend told me to come here," and then he looked down and began to cry.

I helped him complete his Collapse Process, and he was deeply moved at the finish. His heart opened up again for the first time in many years. That night, he went home and dreamed about what he wanted to dedicate the rest of his life to. He didn't know if he had 10, 20, or 30 more years, but life had become precious again, and he didn't want to waste a moment of it. He dreamed that night, and when he came in the next day I helped him get clear on what he loved and had him begin to write down some dreams. All of a sudden, he got inspired. He saw possibilities for himself and his talents where before he'd seen only darkness and a slow shutting down.

At the end of the course, he gave me a hug and a thank you and went on his way, and I heard no more of him until nine months later when I was speaking at a convention in Dallas. About two-thirds of the way through my speech, a door at the back of the room opened, and this same gentleman walked in and sat down in the rear of the auditorium. When I had seen him the first time, he'd been dressed very casually, like a retired man from a small town who had nowhere important to go. But when he came in that day, he was dressed *magnificently.* He was beautifully presented and had a completely different look on his face. He had sharp eyes and vital energy, and there was an unmistakable presence about him.

I finished my talk, signed books, and shook hands, and he just waited until everyone had left. As I approached him, he stood up and asked, "Remember me?"

I said, "Yes, I do. You look different, but I remember you."

He looked me right in the eye, took my hand, and said with a quiet strength, "I'm in business," and I actually choked up.

I was touched because here was a man who'd thought he was *done,* a man who was decaying and about to give up because he'd bought into a collective belief system that says you're supposed to retire at age 65. That belief has nothing to do with the human heart or spirit. It has no basis in anything but an outdated, political idea. He realized he'd swallowed it and scheduled his life around it, and by that unconscious program, he was about to die—not by natural causes, but by beliefs. Then, by a series of what some might call coincidences but are actually universal forces, he came to a seminar, woke up, and turned the lights back on.

He told me he'd joined together with a friend of his own age, a former business associate, and they'd created a successful consulting company that he loves. He has something inspiring to wake up for every morning—people, opportunities, and challenges coming at him every day—which he'd thought he'd never have again because he was just "too old." He looked and felt younger and more vital than he had almost a year before, and he said he was now making more money than he ever did before his retirement. He looked *alive,* and he was inspired about his life. It was deeply moving to me to know a great truth and then see it demonstrated by that man: that the soul of a human being is immortally called to do something magnificent until the body simply can't move another muscle, until it wears out, not rusts out. That driving force never stops, no matter what any person or culture believes.

The Fearful Financier

I've stated that your service to the world and what you're willing to receive for it are the barometers of your self-worth. Well, if you stop work and provide no service, if you don't earn and buy and interact with life by exchanging spirit and matter in all its forms, your self-respect, confidence, and self-worth will plummet. This is a divinely designed fail-safe mechanism to make sure you don't give up on life before it's ready to give up on you. And it applies to everyone, no matter how accomplished they may be.

I once consulted with a man who was the former CEO of one of the world's larger financial institutions. He'd just retired after 30 years of an extremely accomplished and wealthy professional life to become the leader of a well-respected university. The position had a lot of prestige attached, but it was largely honorary, moderately paid, and required some ceremonial and public-relations duties. He walked into my office, and I could immediately sense something beneath his sophisticated surface that just didn't match his appearance. When this gentleman sat down and I asked how I could be of service to him, he suddenly leaned forward with his hands clasped between his knees, his shoulders hunched forward, and an anguished expression on his face.

He blurted out, "I don't *know!* I don't know what the hell's going on. All my life I've been rising and acting so confidently, but suddenly I'm feeling like a nobody. I was a financier, and now I'm the head of a university, but ever since I retired—man, I'm *scared.* It's as if I've been playing a game for 30 years, making people believe I always knew what I was doing, but now I feel like I just don't know, and I'm afraid everyone's going to find out."

I said, "And what would you love to do?"

"I have to find some sort of motivation, something to live for within or in addition to this new position. Ever since I stopped working, I've lost my incentive and drive. I feel like I just . . ." And this powerful leader of international finance almost *cried.*

I said to him, "Do you think you're feeling this way because you're not providing the service you once did for the world and you're not being as economically rewarded? If so, what you're experiencing demonstrates how vital the feeling of productivity is and how fatal inactivity can be. Being of service is one of the most rewarding and life-affirming activities you can do. Providing a service greater than yourself and being rewarded for it is life-generating. I know it feels overwhelming right now, but it can easily be turned around. You spent your whole life being productive and involved, and that's what you were made for. It's time to do what you love and what you're masterful at, and this self-doubt will simply disappear. What would you love to do?"

It's not just what you *have,* it's also what you *do* that impacts what you feel you are, and if you're not doing much, you risk eventually believing that you aren't much. I helped this gentleman find what he would love to do: Share with others within the university the skills he'd mastered over a lifetime for mutual benefit and growth. It didn't take long, because he was burning to get out there and serve once again; he'd just been held back by the illusion that he was supposed to retire.

When we were through, he said, "Thank you, it all makes perfect sense now. I can't believe I was so unaware of such a basic principle of existence. The money isn't really an issue for me now, but man, I needed a *life.*"

The Drive to Be Alive

Not everyone has to descend so far into the perceived loss of confidence and self-worth that so often goes hand in hand with the perceived loss of a meaningful and fulfilling occupation. Some are fortunate enough to get a wake-up call before they retire, and wise enough to heed it.

Some years ago I landed at Boston's Logan Airport and got on the shuttle to the Hilton Hotel where I was teaching. The driver was about 65 years old, and the two of us were alone on his shuttle for the ten-minute drive.

I asked him, "How's it going, sir?" and he answered, "Everything's great thanks."

"Enjoy your job?"

"Oh yeah," and he turned around with a big smile on his face and said, "but I've been here for many years and am about to retire."

I said, "That's great. You know, a secret of life is not to let your retirement get in the way of your work."

He looked at me out of the corner of his eye and said warily, "You don't say!"

"Yes, I do. So what are you going to do when you retire?"

He answered, "Oh, I'm just going to take it easy and relax."

I said, "You know, the statistics show that 18 to 36 months after retirement, many people die if they don't have something to live for, something they love to do. What do you have that's important to live for?"

He became quiet for a moment, and then said, "Well, I'm going to play some golf and do little hobbies and stuff like that."

I said, "Little hobbies make little *people.* If you don't have a purpose to live for that's beyond your present life, your life dissipates. Productivity is one of the secrets of self-worth." He nodded his head in agreement. "Nature never throws away old mechanisms; it just builds new ones on top. You never throw away what you've gained in experience because *none* of it was wasted. There's no such thing as waste. Your whole life was filled with learning experiences to make you a greater being, to build the potential for a greater opportunity to contribute. You have the capacity to be productive until the day you pass from this body."

He became very thoughtful then, maybe even a little deflated. When we arrived at the hotel, he got my bags and said, "You know, young man, you're a very thought-provoking guy. You've really made me stop and think."

I conducted my seminar and didn't return to Boston for more than a year. But when I came back to the same hotel, guess who picked me up? The man was still driving the same shuttle, but there was something different about him: This time he wasn't elated about quitting. He was just present with himself and his work.

As I stood behind him, holding on to the rail, I said, "Remember me? You picked me up a year ago, and we had a conversation about your retirement."

He looked in his mirror and said, "Oooohhh! Oh yeahhh! You're that guy! Let me tell you what happened after we met last time. That night, I went home and I was extremely depressed. I felt so down, in such turmoil, I was in a real identity crisis. That was a night of hell. I talked to my wife and told her what you said about little hobbies and death and life, and she got a tear in her eye."

His wife had been concerned that this was exactly what might happen if he were to retire. Suddenly *he* became afraid of letting his wife down if he didn't retire as they'd always assumed he would. But when he told her his new thoughts, she understood completely. Often a man takes time to learn what a woman's intuition knows immediately. He told me that they'd had this conversation in bed, and she sat there with him as he just cried and cried, because all of a sudden he looked back at his life and woke up to the great question, "What *am* I going to do? Is it possible that I would lose motivation and life without my work? Is this what I really would love to do?"

He'd thought about all the trials and tribulations of his life, his daily tasks and all the people he'd been able to serve at that hotel over so many years. He'd worked there for almost three decades, ever since the elevator had just been a little box on the inside of the building, and he'd seen the entire evolution of the hotel. He remembered all the friends he'd worked with and all the managers he'd served under, the whole mission of the Hilton, all the transformations, and all of the *people,* and he cried.

Just as dawn was breaking at the end of his dark night of the soul, he said to his wife, "I'm afraid that if I retire, something might happen to me, just like that young man said, and I won't be able to spend more years with you. Honey, if I decided not to retire, would you still love me?" And she put her arms around him and *loved* him.

The next day he went to the manager and said, "I know I'm about to retire and we're supposed to be having a party later, but if for some reason I decided not to leave, would I still have a job? Could I still work here? Is it possible that I might not be too old?"

The young manager said to him, "I've only been with the hotel a short time, but from what I've heard, you're a *legend* here. You've got a job as long as you live, my friend."

At that moment, he realized he'd been buying into an illusion, an arbitrarily determined social delusion. Retirement at age 65 is partly a scheme that was fabricated by the government in the 1930s to push older people out of the workforce and create jobs for the young during the Great Depression. It has little to do with the human spirit and capacity. As the population ages and more and more people go on Social Security, the cost is eroding the economy, and the government is reassessing its position. They realize they're not able to replace all the skills, reliability, and experience of senior people, and they're attempting to change the belief system and lift retirement age from 65 to 68-plus because of economics.

When he gave me a ride the second year, that man was inspired about his work. He was more alive and had more vitality than he'd had the year before. He had a vision, and realized that his productivity was his *life*. He said to me, "I'm more alive today than I was a year ago because I have something I really would love to do. I don't want to retire. I want to fulfill this job position possibly until I die. It's been nearly my whole working life. I love the people and the energy, and I realize now that by just hanging around the house I would've driven my wife mad. I *want* to go to work now. I want to produce and serve, and I didn't realize how much I was dying until I decided that I wanted to work again. I can see and feel the difference in myself, and there's no question in my mind that retirement would've been the death of me."

Now he had both the pain and the pleasure of working. I'm sure he had the aches and pains of working at his *age,* but now his purpose was greater than those aches and pains.

May your purpose be greater than your aches and pains. May it be greater than your trials and tribulations, your highs and lows, your age and your youth, even greater than your opinions and beliefs.

I share these stories because, even in youth, you probably don't ask the question at the end of the day: Did I do everything I could with everything I've been given? You don't question what's possible for you, and unless you push the boundaries, you'll never know what you might be capable of.

> *"Experience is not what happens to a man;*
> *it is what a man does with what happens to him."*
>
> — Aldous Huxley

Your Magnificent Mission

I've been exploring human consciousness for more than 31 years, and I'm convinced that there's an immortal part inside of you that calls and directs and pulls you to do something amazing with your life. It might be writing words that will change people's lives, creating music that moves them, committing yourself to a cause that will truly make a difference, finding a cure for humankind's physical or social ills, making a beautiful home or garden, or raising a family with such love and wisdom that the world is a greater place because your children are in it.

Whatever it may be, there's a magnificent mission in everyone, regardless of age. The vitality in every human being is directly proportionate to the vividness of his or her vision. That destiny whispers to you through your intuition and constantly tries to pull you into your heart. It wants you to listen to your inner voice until that voice becomes louder than all opinions and imposed beliefs from the outside, and it guides you to make the contribution that you're uniquely designed to provide to the world. It can take any form, but one of the great joys in life is knowing that you are of service and producing something of value. You can't do something that inspires you without inspiring others. That's a great service to them, and inspiring others inspires you right back and keeps you moving. Fulfillment comes from touching people with your light, not from retirement. And if you honor yourself by listening to your heart, that light will only increase with age.

The Old Fox

There's a law in the universe that says if you don't use it, you lose it. Have you noticed that after about the age of 40, many people use their bodies less and they just start going downhill? Well, the same thing applies to intelligence. The brain is like a muscle, and if you don't use it, it deteriorates. Musicians, athletes, healers, and experts in every field practice constantly to maintain their abilities, and one of your greatest attributes is your mind. When you master the ability to maximize the expression of your spirit through your mind, you approach your true potential. Find the unique quality that is yours and learn how to communicate it to the world, and age can only improve your capacity to reach out and offer some service of immense value.

I once met an elderly man at a hotel in Texas who was lecturing in the room next to where I was speaking. I was drawn by the energy of the people attending his seminar, so I dropped in and introduced myself during one of his breaks. We hit it off immediately, traded life stories, and talked about what inspired us. He was a philanthropist who had made a later-life career out of going to the business and economic faculties of colleges and universities around the country and asking if he could address their students to offer them an unusual business opportunity when they graduated. Once they'd verified his credentials, which were impressive, the schools were delighted to let him speak.

This philanthropic gentleman stood up in front of lecture halls full of young college seniors across America, told them about his experiences, and inspired them by letting them know about the possibilities available in the world of business. Then he'd offer them a business opportunity:

"I'm offering a series of courses. If you attend these courses, study diligently, and fulfill certain requirements, you can receive a reward like nowhere else. The conditions are as follows: You must be in the top 10 percent of your classes, follow an investment plan that I will lay out for you, attend my courses for one year, and do whatever I tell you financially. If you can meet these criteria, at the end of that year I'll help you create a business plan and invest however much money you need in the business of your dreams. I'm prepared to invest any amount— thousands of dollars, hundreds of thousands, *millions* if your plan requires it. But you must guarantee that you'll follow my instructions to the letter for the first three years. I'll extract a certain percentage of the profits, and in return I'll guarantee you an extraordinary return and help you make far more money than you could make without my guidance."

Over and over again, he'd teach young people how to start businesses and make generous profits. He'd take his royalties, then turn around and do it again with the next generation. He was making untold millions of dollars by using his experience to help other people organize their lives in alignment with universal principles and make their own fortunes.

Young people just out of college couldn't possibly have had the wisdom it took him a lifetime to amass, and the ones who followed his instructions far outstripped their peers. He knew the peaks and pitfalls of the commercial world and shared his knowledge gladly. But it was no rescue mission or free handout. He made sure they adhered to the contract. Any who didn't were required to pay him back all his investment money immediately or with interest. He required their discipline and his percentage in return for his mentorship, which kept the arrangement in fair exchange. It was an inbuilt check-and-balance system, and very few who were selected defaulted, because a deal like that is extremely rare. He showed me his book filled with case after case of large companies that he'd been instrumental in starting up through some of the very principles laid out in the book you're reading now. Do you think that this man thought about retirement? Work wasn't a chore to him, it was his *life,* and there was nothing in the world he'd rather do.

As long as you're green, you're growing.
As soon as you're ripe, you rot.

You have a mortal body and an immortal soul, a part of you that's run by the outer world and a part that's inspired from the inner world. Retirement is an illusion of the body, and if you're fooled by it, your body can decay along with your enthusiasm for life. But if you let the immortal part be your guide, nothing on this earth can stop you, because it transcends terrestrial space. Life is not a destination, it's a journey of understanding, service, and mastery, and there's no end to your growth.

Some people say, "When I finally get to a certain point, I'm going to be fulfilled and happy, and I'll be *done.*" What they're working toward is possibly dementia or a stroke. There's a strong connection between what you think and what happens to you. As a spiritual being, you're meant to eternally grow and evolve, and you'll never be "done."

When your life is a fulfilling adventure, why would you want it to be over? Are you here simply to have an ending? Or are you here for a magnificent and un-retiring journey? If you don't use your body, mind, and spirit continually and creatively, they can break down. As long as you're fulfilling an inspiring service that you love, you'll have a desire to live. You may leave a particular career and go on to do something else, but don't retire from life. Find a mission that will fulfill you for the rest of your existence. As long as you draw breath and have something meaningful to do, you'll continue to be a lifelong inspirational force for yourself and anyone fortunate enough to meet you. Heaven on Earth isn't bounded by time, it's what you carry in your heart when you live a full life of service and meaning, and it need not end until you do.

Exercise

This is called the Perfect Day Exercise. It's a preparation for living your life according to your highest heavenly vision.

If you could have an entire day filled with nothing but your most inspiring activities and dreams, what would it look like? Sit down with your journal and write out your perfect day exactly as you would most love it to be. Schedule an entire 24 hours from the moment you wake up, whether it be 4 A.M. or noon. Have the sleep you want, see the sunrise or sunset from some beautiful place, eat the perfect breakfast, meditate, run, swim, exercise, study, have a massage, garden, dance, write, sing, travel, teach, serve, work, consult, speak, make love, dream, play . . . this is your day. Whatever that perfect day is for you, map it out, pick a date, commit to doing it, and then go fulfill it.

First plan it for once a year, and once you've done that and realized it's possible, raise the number to four times a year—once per season. Then go to once a month, and then work toward having a perfect day every single week. Increase the frequency until eventually almost every day of your life is lived in accord with your dreams.

Let yourself go with this exercise. It's an amazing opportunity to think about what you love doing, and then to find out you have the capacity to make it happen. This is a day dedicated to doing exactly what your heart would love. If you don't schedule it, who will?

This is a wonderful formula for gradually building the life of your dreams, one that you'll slowly come to realize you actually deserve. Don't be surprised if your idea of a perfect day evolves over time to include more service, because you're training yourself to do what you love and love what you do and be of service to others. When you discover and provide the service you love, your life becomes fulfilling.

Words of Wisdom and Power

- *The light of my spirit burns brighter with age.*

- *My service is my life, and my life truly works.*

- *I serve, and then I serve some more, and boy, is my life rewarding!*

- *Little actions make little lives, big actions make big lives, and my actions are gigantic.*

- *The service I provide and the work I love stand way beyond any form of retirement.*

- *I do everything I can with everything I am given.*

Chapter Eleven
The Power of Relationship

"When you love you should not say, 'God is in my heart,'
but rather, 'I am in the heart of God.' And think not
that you can direct the course of love, for love, if it finds
you worthy, directs your course."

— Kahlil Gibran

YOU'VE SEEN that highly volatile emotions can dissipate wealth. But what can elicit such wobbly emotions more than unloving or unfulfilling relationships? Emotionally charged relationships can dissipate your potential to amass heavenly fortunes. Your heart is your greatest asset. It's the source of your inspiration and love and the connection to your divine soul. Investing in a loving heart can save you time, energy, and wealth. People spend a great amount of time and money learning how to master business, but they never consider learning how to conduct caring relationships. As a result, many people don't know the art of loving.

In business, you reach the Peter Principle of incompetence the minute you have emotions about people—about hiring or firing, confronting or supporting them. Emotions halt your growth in that area, and the same thing applies to relationships. In relationships, you reach the Peter Principle of incompetence the minute you're infatuated with, or resent, others. When you place someone on a pedestal or in the pit and emotionally react, your emotions will run your life and potentially your wealth until you bring them back into the balanced, center point of love and appreciation. Marriage is a 50/50 proposition—half don't last for life, and an acrimonious divorce can cost you at least 50 percent of everything you've worked so hard and long to create. Yet the quest for love is as urgent and powerful as the quest for wealth. Wouldn't it be wise to invest some effort into making sure you're as skillful in the one as you are in the other?

Both positive and negative emotions dissipate love and wealth because both are blinding and lead to distorted reactions. When relationships break down, you can diminish your business, your wealth, your health, and your heart. Mastering the ability to choose, maintain, or end relationships is as crucial to growing and retaining your wealth as mastering financial principles. So let's explore the illusions, lessons, and truth about relationships, and save your heart and your heavenly fortune.

The Fantasy

The basic fantasy that creates volatile emotions is the belief in one-sidedness, the search for positive without negative or pleasure without pain. You may think you want soft without hard, but if you attempt to raise a child with nothing but support, ease, and softness, you can make it dependent and weak. Instead, if you give it challenge, difficulty, and toughness, it can become strong. A child requires both sides, because the maximum development of human beings occurs at the border of chaos and order, or challenge and support. True love is that center point or balanced synthesis of the two, and that's exactly what every person consciously or unconsciously receives. As long as you keep looking for one side instead of embracing the whole two-sided person, you'll experience the other side all the more intensely. If you attempt to live in a fantasy, you'll become frustrated and disillusioned with people because you'll keep trying to make them match your fantasy, and it's not going to happen. Anything you infatuate with, you'll keep dealing with until you get the message.

Many years ago I had a client in New York who was one of the wealthier women in the city. She'd written an exact and exhaustive list of the qualities of her ideal man, and it ran like this: "I won't even *date* a man unless he has a minimum of $15 million, is at least 6'1", has brown hair and eyes, owns a large company, is socially prominent, has at least one beautiful house, loves the finest in everything, is utterly devoted to pampering me, is willing to massage me at night . . ." Her list was all positives without any negatives, on and on. She had a list that no human being could ever fulfill.

I said, "Rachael, I've seen your criteria, and I don't think such a man exists."

She said, "That's just because *you* don't measure up. *I'll* find him." She was looking for an idealized, Hollywood version of *her fantasy,* but what she kept attracting into her life were the disowned parts she didn't want anything to do with. She kept attracting gigolos with no job or money who wanted her to support them, who deceived her with big stories, used drugs, and had sex with her and then her friends. They were the virtual opposite of her fantasy. What they had going for them was strong physical and sexual attractiveness. She kept falling for them, believing each time that the right man had finally come along or that she could change them into her ideal.

This scenario had been going on for a number of years. Then I received a call from her two years ago: "Dr. Demartini! Is there any way you can come to Hawaii for my wedding? I've finally found my man!"

I said, "Really? I'm booked in Europe and can't make it, but congratulations!" In the back of my mind I was thinking, *I've got to meet this guy.* Sometime later, I was giving a seminar in California and bumped into her in a fine resort hotel. "So Rachael," I asked, "how's married life?"

"Oh . . . well . . . it didn't work out."

"But I thought he was the man of your dreams."

"Ahhh . . . he turned out to be another bastard. Gotta go. Bye!"

She didn't want to talk about it, but what she had done was become infatuated and put another man on the pedestal, and then put him in the pit. Her infatuated blindness lifted him up too high, then put him down too low when he didn't match the fantasy.

You can't have a meeting of the heart with anyone you place above or below you; they must be right there *with* you. Otherwise, you don't have a relationship, you have a fantasy that's guaranteed to be shattered. I call these hidden affairs.

So many men and women have romantic fantasies. Some women have them about the knight in shining armor who scoops them up in his arms with a rose in his teeth and carries them off to his castle/penthouse for mad, passionate lovemaking. What they get is a guy with a big belly who scratches his butt, who's just being a guy. But they *punish* him for it because he doesn't match their fantasy. The guys have a fantasy that the girl is supposed to be beautiful, sexy, nurturing, and stay 30 years old for the rest of her life. They punish or leave her for being human. It costs them love if they stay and money if they go.

Fantasy stories and fairy tales have torments to balance their pleasures. We elevate and then torture others and ourselves because of unreal or impossible fantasies. Embracing both sides is essential. Otherwise, we'll experience the extreme highs and lows of the emotional swings instead of balanced love.

The Teacher

The more extreme the illusion you create, the more intense and costly the lesson. *The very strength of attraction in a relationship based on infatuation becomes equal to the strength of repulsion and resentment that occurs when the other person doesn't match up to your fantasy.* Infatuations are balanced by resentments, and pleasure by pain. Together they make up the path to true love.

I was sitting in a restaurant in New York City one evening with my wife and a friend of hers when another lady raced over to our table with great excitement. She said, "I've met the man of my dreams! He's *perfect.* He's incredibly wealthy, he has a huge yacht, he's handsome and charming and romantic . . ." I just sat there nodding and smiling and saying, "That's great!"

The lady sitting with us had already dated the man and knew how it was going to end, but she didn't have the heart to tell her. My wife was squeezing my leg under the table as if to say, "*Don't* you say a word."

The man was a wealthy playboy whose life consisted of sailing around the world from city to city, picking up beautiful women. He'd invite them onto his yacht and into his life, take them to the most exclusive places and give them expensive gifts, be there every minute for two or three weeks of intense honeymoon passion and romance . . . and then just move on. Suddenly he was gone, or wouldn't return their calls, and the fairy tale was over. Some women had actually attempted suicide when it happened to them. Was he an evil man? No, he was there to teach these women about romantic infatuations. And they were there to teach *him,* because men like that have to deal with women seeking their revenge in a fatal attraction. One extreme attracts the other, and they come together to teach each other lessons in love.

I saw that lady three weeks later and she was *devastated,* almost suicidal, because she had given up her life to this guy for three weeks and now he was gone. She was sick to her stomach; had headaches; and was angry, introverted, and depressed. Her resentment was so extreme that she actually wanted his blood. All of it was just a measure of her infatuation with the image she thought had been stolen from her. For three weeks, her infatuation had been so distracting she could barely work, and then for another three weeks she was so resentful she was virtually useless at her job.

Have you ever been so infatuated or resentful of someone that you couldn't get them out of your mind and couldn't even think about work? Did you know that the inefficiencies and ineffectiveness in businesses are primarily due to the oscillations of infatuation and resentment going on in the lives of the people who work there? It's called lower productivity, in business and in life. People who are present are more productive, and the only way to be present is to see things as they truly are, not as you imagine them to be.

It was a hard lesson, but my wife's friend probably won't give her heart to a fantasy so easily again. Maybe she's learned to look deeper. Your wealth flows in and out, up and down, according to your presence, and during emotional extremes the tide is definitely down and out.

*Holding a grudge is like drinking poison
and hoping someone else will die.*

Values

Have you ever been in a relationship where you tried to change your mate? If you self-righteously tell someone they're wrong and try to fix them, they'll fight you, dig in, and do whatever annoys you even more. That's because their *values* are different from yours. Values are what's important to you, what you dedicate your time, energy, and money to. Commonly, the man will have the values of career, finance, and mental or rational development, and the woman will be focused on relationship, social life, health, and beauty. This isn't chauvinism, because they aren't male or female characteristics, they're *masculine* or *feminine* traits. We all have both, but we tend to express one side and repress the other, and the more you're polarized to either side, the more probable it is that your partner will be polarized to the other.

A highly motivated man who's totally focused on the masculine side will more likely attract a woman who's equally focused on the feminine side, because she's his complementary balance. They're attracted together *because* they're different, and their relationship creates wholeness and balance in their extremes. That's the divine order, but usually each of them tries to get the other to live according to their values. They're infatuated with their similarities and resentful of their differences, unaware that the core of the relationship actually is those very differences— that's where the challenge and growth are found. If they got their wish for similarity, they'd get bored with each other. If any two people are exactly the same, one of them is unnecessary.

Relationships exist to expand you by pushing your buttons about the things you haven't yet loved. The ideal relationship isn't comfortable and easy, it's one that gives you exactly the number of buttons you can tolerate. If you get more than you can handle, you burn out; but if you get too few, you become bored, and boredom or burnout eventually ends the relationship.

There's no such thing as a completely trusting relationship; that's just another fantasy. If the man's higher values are money and career, then whenever his business is threatened he'll leave his lower values to take care of the higher ones. If the woman's highest values are family and health, when her children are sick she'll immediately drop work to be with them. He expresses his love by making sure the money is there to support them all, and she expresses hers by being there for whoever needs her. The two together make up love. They're both expressing love through their values, and no two people have exactly the same ones. You can trust your partner to be true to his or her own values and take care of the part of life you're less focused on, and you'll do the same, and *that's* the trust. You can only truly trust others to live their values, not yours—unless, of course, you sell them on your values. But that's up to you, not them.

No matter how much you try to be selfless, half the time you'll be focused on your own values. You have your own life, and if you try to sacrifice it for another, they'll take you for granted and put you down because that's what you're doing to yourself. That means you're going to challenge and betray and resent them at times, and they'll do the same to you. That's *normal.* If you don't understand this, you'll feel betrayed every time they choose to honor their values over yours. You may think that your love is broken when that happens, but the truth is that your love has just begun, because pleasure and pain together make up true love. Every relationship has honesty and dishonesty, trust and betrayal, closeness and distance. That's what a balanced life is about. If you're honest with yourself for a moment, you'll discover that you can't be honest with yourself at all times, nor always be trusted. Why would you expect others to always be one-sided? Maximum evolution occurs with a balance of support and challenge, and when you give that to each other, you have a loving and fulfilling relationship. If you don't, you'll get a lesson.

Betrayal

I consulted with a gentleman in Europe, a successful entrepreneur who was passionately attracted to a girl 15 years his junior. As he spoke about her, it was obvious that he was living in a fantasy: "She's so sweet and good and beautiful; she's absolutely pure pleasure." I attempted to alert him to a possible other side of equal intensity that he hadn't seen yet, but he wouldn't hear of it. Then she became pregnant, and his values were suddenly and deeply challenged. He tried to get her to have an abortion, but she was quite religious and wouldn't consider it. Suddenly he saw her as purely negative—he only saw the side he hadn't been willing to look at before: "She's not very ambitious, she's needy, she doesn't have any wealth, she's unsophisticated, she costs a lot, she's going to lose her beauty, she's having a baby . . ."

He felt trapped, and he was angry with *her* for trapping him. I told him that she hadn't trapped him, he'd trapped *himself* by his unwillingness to see both sides, by his refusal to believe that every relationship has both pain and pleasure equally. He'd had a fantasy of pleasure without pain, and then he had the opposite nightmare of pain without pleasure. It happened because he was driven by his passionate desires and emotions and didn't wisely ask himself, "What am I doing here? Is this someone to have a fling with, or someone I could really love?" When she became pregnant, he woke up to all their incompatibilities related to morals, careers, religion, finances—all the things he hadn't seen before because he'd been blinded by infatuation.

I explained to him that she and the baby were his teachers, because from this point on, he would seldom forget that, despite appearances, everything has two sides. He thought she'd betrayed him. In truth, she'd liberated him from an illusion and a fear. What he'd most feared—accountability, or what some call commitment—was the very thing he'd have to face because he would love his child. Was he a victim? No. Was he learning a lesson in love? Yes.

Polarities

Lessons can be accomplished either by bringing people together or by breaking them apart. I recently worked with a couple in Oklahoma who learned that lesson the hard way. The wife was obsessed with teaching their four children; she kept them at home and taught them all day. Her polarity was addiction to the children, so his was to work most of the time and do whatever he could to stay out of the house. He was partly sick of the kids.

Anytime one partner goes to an extreme, the other will commonly go in the opposite direction. All her energy and affection was directed to the children, and she believed that her husband only cared about money and business. She thought that he should be home more; he thought that she should be out there working more, and both polarities were unrealistic fantasies opposing each other to neutralize the illusion and open them up to the value of the other side.

He ended up having an affair, and that's when I was called in to help them sort things out. I showed him how his rejection of home life had fueled her obsession with it, and I showed her how her extreme focus on family had fueled his desire to be out of it, and how the affair happened to wake them up and value each other more. If they see it, they'll get the lesson and grow together. She'll understand the importance of giving some attention to him, his work, and finances, and he'll spend more time appreciating the children. If they stubbornly refuse to see the order, they'll go through a divorce and maybe get the lesson that way. She'll have to think about making a living and being out of the house, he'll start missing the children, and they'll learn to appreciate each other's values.

You'll probably partly specialize in one area or another, but it's wise to know something about all seven areas of life (spiritual, mental, vocational, financial, social, familial, and physical) in order to have a relationship based on sharing rather than dependence. Emotion and ignorance seek one-sidedness. Love and wisdom know that there are two sides to every issue. Any conflict subsides if you can stop, reflect, and say, "I see and honor you for who you are. I realize you're there to teach me about the parts of myself I've been ignoring and make me a more complete person. Thank you." If you can speak from your heart, your partner will go into his or her heart and meet you in the center. When you stop trying to change the other person, in that moment they'll transform. The light of that wisdom unites polarities, but the longer you refuse to get the lesson, the more time and money it costs you. The lesson is love, and if you wake up to it, you may not leave.

"People are like stained glass windows: they sparkle and shine when the sun is out, but when the darkness sets in, their true beauty is revealed only if there is a light from within."
— Elisabeth Kübler-Ross

Caring and Selling

Has anyone ever said to you, "I'm not getting enough out of this relationship"? If so, they were telling you that, in their perceptions, you weren't meeting their needs and fulfilling their values. When that happens, they start looking elsewhere. Is that callous? No, it's making sure you appreciate and honor those who come into your life. Outside of relationships it's called *selling,* but inside relationships it's called *caring*. Caring and selling are actually identical; they both mean knowing and meeting people's values. Don't fool yourself about this. A relationship is a buying-and-selling proposition. To raise your value in the relationship marketplace, you must know the other person's values and figure out how to fulfill them. If you can't do that, *you* have little or no value. They're sharing their life with you, and the instant they feel strongly enough that they're not getting value for their investment, they'll go somewhere else, just like your clients.

Haven't you seen older, wealthy men with younger, beautiful women? That's an example of compatible values of wealth and beauty meeting each other. They wouldn't be together if they both weren't having their values fulfilled. Money and beauty are powerful forces in the relationship marketplace, and if you don't have one, it helps to have the other. To think otherwise is just another fantasy. The same thing happens in nature. For penguins, rocks symbolize power and value. If you go to New York City's Central Park Zoo during the penguin mating season, you'll see large male penguins standing proudly next to their big piles of rocks, while the puny little penguins have a few pathetic stones. There's a real hierarchy there; the female penguins walk up and down, checking them out, and the more stones a male has, the more beautiful mates he attracts. The smaller, weaker penguins don't get any rocks or mates. The ability to provide value leads to natural selection in the eyes of any given species.

We humans are more sophisticated, so our range of value is greater. We look for qualities such as intelligence, love, humor, and wealth, but the principle still holds. The more you can maximize and express your finest qualities in a form that others can appreciate, the more they'll want to be with you. True love involves knowing and respecting your loved one's values, and expressing your values in terms of theirs. If you don't honor them by knowing what's important to them and how to provide it, you don't know how to care about them. There's no such thing as, "Now that I have my partner, I can take him or her for granted." You're responsible for maintaining fair exchange, even in your relationships. A relationship is an ongoing sales process, a constantly renewable contract on invisible paper, so live up to your side of the contract.

"All that is not given is lost."

— Pali Scripture

Separate Lives

I recommend that a husband and wife have partially separate assets. Many people find this quite shocking, but whether you divorce or stay together, it's wise to make a list of all your assets, allocate what goes to whom, and update it regularly. Why? For one reason, you're already doing it in your head anyway. On a subconscious level, you think you own *this* and they think they own *that*. It's common sense to remove all uncertainty; otherwise, it's just repressed. Only someone out of exchange and fearfully clinging to a relationship would resist doing this, but it really helps to get clear and maintain fair exchange.

I just worked with a married couple, and I consulted with the husband first. He wanted to total up their individual and joint assets, but his wife was a little apprehensive until I spoke with her. She didn't understand why he'd want to do such a thing.

I asked her, "Do you believe you deserve to know what you've earned or own during your time together?"

She said, "Well, yes. I guess I do."

"And would you like to know your exact financial value in this marriage?"

"Yes, I would."

So we totaled it up and I said, "Right now you have $100,000 worth of assets sitting here." When I presented it that way, it took on a new meaning for her.

She said, "Oh! You mean, those are sort of . . . mine?" And she had a new appreciation of herself and the marriage, an increased self-worth that was invaluable.

For the same reason, you may have a desire to keep as yours some of the things you bring into the marriage. The purpose of this exercise is not to divorce or separate, but to identify the total assets and find out what's considered yours, what's considered your spouse's, and what has been unconsciously decided.

In addition to having a joint account, it's also wise for a husband and wife to have their own separate accounts. If one partner works and makes all the money, and the other works at keeping the house and raising the kids, the one who isn't being paid for their work doesn't know their value and may have an increased tendency to overspend and blow money, or underspend and hoard it.

I worked this out with a doctor and his wife awhile ago. He made a substantial amount of money and controlled it all, while she raised the kids and got zero. There was plenty of money for food, clothing, and luxuries, but she didn't have any that was hers alone, and she felt *devalued*. As a result, she blew large amounts of money out of unconscious fear, resentment, and compensation for her uncertain worthiness.

I said to him, "All right, if your wife died, how much would it cost every month to hire a nurse, maid, and cook to do everything she does?"

"Uh . . . $4,400."

"Okay, you're going to pay her $4,400 a month, but out of that she has to pay a portion of the rent, the babysitter, and so on. She can keep her spending money, but she has responsibilities with the rest." They both ended up with more money. She immediately stopped blowing as much money and frittering away their nest egg because she realized she had a value, a net worth in their relationship. She'd been contributing tremendously all along, but her contribution had gone unrecognized.

There can be many unspoken tensions in a marriage around money, because money also represents power, and everyone wants theirs. If you don't feel you have the freedom to do what you love, you'll resent each other, so it's smart to have common freedoms. Any lack of honor, worth, or freedom will impact your wealth and relationship, so stay aware and keep growing.

"Love one another, but make not a bond of love . . .
Give your hearts, but not into each other's keeping.
For only the hand of life can contain your hearts.
And stand together yet not too near together:
For the pillars of the temple stand apart,
And the oak and the cypress grow not in each other's shadow."

— Kahlil Gibran

The Heart of the Matter

There are lessons of love that can be learned in coming together and in going apart. I knew a gentleman in the southwestern United States a number of years ago who was involved in a knock-down, drag-out divorce that lasted for two solid years. He was an oil tycoon, one of the wealthiest people in his state. He and his wife were fighting bitterly, running up *millions* of dollars in legal fees, and the media was eating it up.

I told him, "When you're ready to resolve this conflict, just call me."

He said, "Ah, it's all too complex and difficult."

Eventually he became ill, and his new lady said to him, "You promised you'd be with me, but it's been two years now and I can't stand this much more. I'm thinking about leaving you."

He was afraid he'd lose it all—his money, his relationship, and his health—so at last he said, "All right, John. Now I'll talk to you."

I sat him down in my office and made him write down a list of every single thing he judged about his wife: She wanted something for nothing, she was no good, she treated him badly . . . he wrote a long list of negative qualities. But when I said, "Now it's important to do the same with her positives," he couldn't come up with more than two or three. "But you married her!" I said. "How could you marry someone without positive qualities?"

"Well, she had 'em once, but not anymore," he said. This is an illusion, since we never really lose any qualities, we just change their forms, but he just couldn't see her positive traits. So instead, I had him own every single trait he saw in her. Where had *he* done the same things in his own life? Where had *he* been vindictive? Where had *he* taken money? Where had *he* wanted something for nothing? Where had *he* been vengeful? Who saw *him* as he saw her? Whom had *he* cheated?

He found that everything he saw in her, he also had in himself. He humbled himself to the truth and saw how he was just like her in his own ways. That freed up his mind a little, and he was then able to see more of her positives until they equaled the negatives. He eventually balanced out the slate.

When we looked at the benefits of each one of his wife's negative traits and how they had *served* him, he was astonished. He sat there with tears in his eyes, finally realizing how much of his business success and wealth he owed to his wife. He had never, ever acknowledged that fact in his whole life. He was no longer frightened or angry or guilty. He was humble, present, grateful, certain, and loving.

In that moment I asked, "How do you feel about your wife now?"

He said, "I had no idea. I never saw how much she contributed to my life. She deserves far more than she's asking for. She earned it."

The lawyers had said to them, "Don't talk to each other! Stay away or you'll mess up the whole deal!" In other words, the lawyers would lose their fees. But he went to see her with a humble heart. She opened the door, he walked in and sat down with her, and he read to her all the things she'd done for him. He thanked her for her strength, her love and support, her insights into his partners, her ideas, her social connections that had opened doors for him . . . a long list filled with gratitude. She listened in silence until he finished, and she was brought to tears because all she'd really wanted was to be *appreciated* for her contribution to his life.

So he cried, and she cried, and he turned to her and asked, "What would you like?" She told him what she felt was fair, and it wasn't even half of what he was willing to give her. She didn't want it! Like every human being, she mainly wanted to be acknowledged and loved, and to feel that she'd contributed to his life. She didn't want to be put on a pedestal or in a pit. She just wanted to be put in his heart. She desired to know that, no matter what happened, love would always be there. That's our truest nature. They settled the divorce that week. They'd been consumed with emotional turmoil and illusion, and love came in and swept it all away.

I met his new lady afterward, and she didn't say much. She just put her arms around me and said, "Thank you. I deeply love this man, and I was beginning to think I would never have him, or that we'd have to deal with his wife for the rest of our lives. When he came home and told me about his gratitude for her, I respected him even more. I thought, *If she can put him through all that and he still loves her, then no matter what I do, he'll love me.*

The truth saved him a fortune in legal fees because he then had the clarity to tell his lawyers exactly what he wanted. Your legal counselors are often reflections of you: If you're uncertain, they'll throw every one of your fears out on the table to make sure you face them, and they'll charge you a bundle for the privilege. The minute you're certain about what you'd love, they'll enact it without hesitation. The truth not only saved his money, his relationships, and his health, it saved his *life.* He was only in his 50s, but his anger and bitterness were so overwhelming that he was headed for a heart attack. When you attack or deny your own heart, it attacks you right back.

Anything you love, you have the power to transform. No matter how emotional you are about someone, deep down inside you still love. That's the truth. Instead of oscillating between infatuation and resentment, why not open your heart to the balance in all people? Wake up to their magnificence, because it's the truth, and the truth sets you free for heavenly wealth.

> "A woman is the only thing I am afraid of that
> I know will not hurt me."
>
> — Abraham Lincoln

True Spiritual Love

The loving union of male and female makes up a powerful link-age of spiritual forces, forming a whole that's much greater than the sum of the parts. Love is a powerful magnetic force. As you open the doors of your heart and release the magnificent worthiness that patiently waits within, love draws people, opportunities, and wealth to you in an increasing flood. When you appreciate and work with the energies of the opposite side in yourself and in your partner, tremendous light and power are born.

Mastery of relationships is vital to the mastery of wealth because, ultimately, others simply reflect and represent your relationship with yourself. Unless you love you, you won't love them and vice versa. Love is divine, and when you're in love, you're in the heavenly state. Heaven is right here and right now, the gate is in your own heart, and love is the key to all the treas-ures of spirit and matter. Use the key.

Exercise 1

The definition of *caring* is the same as *selling,* so being in a caring relationship means being a caring salesperson. If you don't know how to sell yourself, if you don't know your value, don't expect to maintain a quality relationship. Your relationships reflect your self-image, and unless you're certain of your value, you'll find it challenging to sell others on being with you.

Make a list—a *long* list—of all the qualities and strengths you have to offer. You're an immortal spirit with every magnificent human quality in your own unique form. Don't spend time thinking small and putting yourself down lower than you truly are, or exaggerating higher. Just awaken to your true and pow-erful qualities that are worthy of love. Continue listing your qual-ities and strengths until you can say, "Damn, I truly *am* worthy of love!" If you can't sell yourself to yourself, why would some-one else buy you? Then care enough to communicate your val-ues in terms of other people's values.

Exercise 2

Having love and appreciation for yourself is vital, but it's only half the equation. Now make a list of all your partner's qualities, all the traits you appreciate and feel grateful for, and don't stop until you get a tear in your eye and feel your partner in your heart. It's easier than you may think. When you can truly feel your partner, make a list of what's important to him or her. In this state of openheartedness, it will be much clearer to you— you'll just know.

Beside each value, write down five ways that you can fulfill it for your partner in a meaningful way by expressing your values. If you're already doing it, how can you do it more effectively? And if you're not doing it, how can you begin?

The amazing thing is that when you care for someone in this way, they spontaneously start doing it in return. You receive what you broadcast.

Words of Wisdom and Power

- *I am skillful in the art of loving relationships, so I keep building my profits.*

- *I transcend my grudges and am grateful for my lessons.*

- *I expect no one to live by my values but me.*

- *When I speak from my heart, people hear it in theirs.*

- *I know my partner's values, and I speak in terms of them.*

- *I do not put the ones I love on a pedestal or in a pit; I put them in my heart.*

Chapter Twelve
The Power
of Purpose

"When you are inspired by some great purpose . . .
your mind transcends limitations, and your consciousness
expands in all directions. . . . Dormant forces, faculties, and
talents become alive, and you discover yourself to be a greater
person by far than you ever dreamed yourself to be."

— Patanjali

YOU WERE born with a magnificent purpose to fulfill in this world; buried deep in your heart, it's your reason for being. When you awaken to your purpose, you're inspired. Your enthusiasm and energy create a magnificent life in accord with the dream and vision that are the gifts of your soul.

We've been exploring many ways of increasing heavenly wealth, but if you don't have a *purpose* for it, an inspiring cause, you won't remain driven toward your fullest potential. Your heavenly wealth is proportionate to what you intend to do with it. Little causes attract little wealth, great causes attract great wealth, and immortal causes attract vast wealth.

The point of a purpose is to give you such a big "why" for your life that you attract the resources, money, and people to help you overcome any obstacle on the path to your dream. When the whys are big enough, the hows take care of themselves. Those with great purpose have the courage and discipline to go beyond their fears, to act with inspiration, to go even beyond *themselves* and what they think is possible. Those who don't, don't. So if your *why* isn't big enough, you won't do what you know in your heart you're capable of. If you don't fill your garden with flowers, it fills up with weeds. If you don't fill your life with what you love, it will fill up with what you don't.

To the degree that you remain unconscious of your purpose, someone else will partly determine your destiny. You'll be told what to do, and you'll get weeds instead of flowers. Anything you don't decide will be decided for you. So decide whether you'd love to live your own life or let others to run it for you. That's the difference between a leader and a follower: One listens to the soul and leads, the other is afraid to listen and follows.

You have a mortal and an immortal self, a part that's run by the outer world and a part that's inspired from the inner world. If you allow your mortal self to run your life, you're like sand blowing in the wind and you leave little or no trace in this world. If you let the immortal part inspire and direct you, you're like a mountain, and the world can't move you. Lives that are outer-directed and disorganized are powerless, but lives that are inner-directed and focused have tremendous power. So let's look at how to find and implement your greatest possible why.

"He who has a big enough why can bear any how."
— Friedrich Nietzsche

You Do Know Your Purpose

I work almost every day with people who say they don't know what they'd love to do, but I've found this not to be true. I say to them, "In your heart you know exactly what you'd love to do, but the fears and guilt in your head stop you from acknowledging it." I then break it down so they can approach what they'd love without the fears paralyzing their vision. I start with the most obvious questions: "Would you love to eat quality food?"

"Of course."

"Great, write that down. What else is ridiculously easy to say you'd love to do?"

"Well, I'd love to travel."

I build on what they *know* they'd love and let it unfold: "Would you love to be wealthy? How wealthy? Where and when would you love to travel? Would you love to make a difference in the world? Okay, in what way? Would you love to write, paint, speak, build, or teach? What inspires you most? Would you love to work with people? When we put all those criteria together, what are the possibilities?" You may not know the details consciously, but inside your soul, it's all perfectly clear and just waiting for you to call on it. So start with what you do know and build.

I worked with a gentleman in France who stated categorically, "I have absolutely no idea what I want to do with my life."

I told him, "Well, I have absolute certainty that you do, and if you don't determine the direction of your life, someone else will, so I'm going to decide for you right now. You'll be a chimney sweep."

"No, that's certainly not it."

"Great, we've ruled out one of 42,000 possibilities. Let's keep going. I want you to work as a prostitute in the poorest quarter of Paris."

"Of course not!"

"Then you'll sell packets of chewing gum in Mexico."

"No."

"Hairstylist and toupee salesman to bald men?"

"No, no, no!"

"All right, if you know what it *isn't,* then you obviously know something about what it *is.* What is it? If you knew you could fulfill it, what would it be?" I took him from the ridiculous to the sublime, and out it came. He had a great dream in his heart, but he was afraid it was too big for him. The only thing stopping him from expressing it was his fear . . . and you may be the same. If you *knew* you could fulfill it, if your fairy godmother could wave her wand and guarantee its fulfillment, what would you most love to do with your life?

The truth is that you know what you'd love to do, but you may not know *how* to do it. You might be banging your head against the wall trying to do it, or avoiding it until you eventually say, "I really wouldn't love to do it." When people say that they wouldn't love to do what really inspires them, it just means they haven't figured out a strategy to do it. If you don't know how to fulfill what you'd love in life, you'll lie to yourself that you don't know your purpose or wouldn't love it, because the pains seem to outweigh the pleasures. But what if you discovered that you could receive the most fulfilling pay for doing what you'd truly love more than anything else in the world? One way to do it is by breaking your purposeful doing into manageable steps.

God Is in the Details

One of the top architects in America, an ingenious man who designs many of the skyscrapers of New York, starts his masterpieces with the broad basics and then keeps refining. A single project may take years, but by the time he's done, he knows every single bolt, every yard of carpet, the dimensions of every wall, and how much paint he'll need. He's at the top of his field because he sees every detail with extreme clarity, and his work flows more smoothly.

Whatever your dream is, take the time to work it out in great detail. Any detail you can't see and leave out of your vision becomes an obstacle or challenge you'll attract or face, and the obstacles are designed to help you clarify your vision. A great question is, is your life worth masterfully planning the details? The Great Designer designed you with nearly infinite detail or you wouldn't have survived. Is your purposeful dream, which comes from the same source, worth any less? Presence is nothing more than approaching an infinity of detail. The greater your details, the greater your presence, and the more power you have to magnetically draw opportunities and resources. Failing to plan is planning to fail, but if you take the time to define and refine exactly what you'd love to be, do, and have in your life, that's what begins to appear.

You brush your teeth several times daily. That's about five minutes for such a small task. What if you devoted the same amount of time every day to discovering, refining, and fulfilling your purpose? What impact could that five minutes per day have on your life if you disciplined yourself to sit down and ask, "What exactly would I love to dedicate or devote my life to? What's my purpose?"

Some people say, "I don't bother planning, because if you want God to laugh, just tell him your plans," but that's not exactly wise or true. Of course you'll have challenges along the way, but it's a simple fact that those who plan their lives, their careers, and their finances go further and end up with more life and wealth than those who don't. The same principle applies to your life. If you would love a life that conforms to your highest dream and vision, you're responsible to be clear about what that is. A detailed plan allows your mind to know what's possible, which removes some of the fear. It removes doubt, adds certainty, and puts you in a resonance that attracts new opportunities.

How can the universe provide you what you would love if you don't have the trust and courage to declare and ask for it? I wonder what the world would be like if parents gave as much attention to helping their children clarify their purpose in life as they do to getting them to brush their teeth. What if parents asked, "Johnny, what would you love your destiny to be? What would you love to devote your life to?"

Every time you say, "I don't know what my purpose is, I don't have that capacity," you prolong the time you spend not doing what you love. Don't empower those personas, those masks covering your true and more enlightened nature. No one else can give you your purpose, because you were born with it. You *do* know what your mission is, so treat yourself like a monarch and ask, "What shall we do with the kingdom today, your majesty?" and decide it in detail.

Space and Time

Goals and purpose are by no means the same thing. To own a business and make $500,000 a year is a goal. To dedicate your life to the study and mastery of universal laws is a lifelong purpose. Goals are the mortal objectives you set for yourself; they're stepping-stones you accomplish along the path of your immortal journey. A purpose isn't something you accomplish, it's something you *live,* and there's no end to it. A goal may be within your life; a purpose is through or beyond it. Fulfilling goals along the journey of your purpose will encourage you, and an inspiring purpose will give meaning to your achievements. Senility and decay are not often an issue for people with a profound purpose. A great purpose allows you to achieve great goals. You live and work as if you were immortal, and that momentum maintains your vitality right through to the end.

The magnitude of the space and time horizons within your innermost dominant thoughts determines the level of conscious evolution you've obtained. Inspired beings have big dreams. They think in long time frames and draw power from their visions. Short time frames have less power.

In a large and bustling city, you could run into an ambitious young person just beginning her career, almost begging for money to survive, living hand-to-mouth and day-to-day. If you ask her how it's going, she'll say, "It's been a fine day," or "It's been a rough day."

If you speak to the same person one year later, she may now be living week-to-week and say, "It's been a fair week," or "It's been a challenging week." If you talk to this person a year later, "It's been a great month" may be her reply, and then two years later, "It's been a fabulous year."

Five years later this same person could say, "I've had a couple of blessed years, and in the next five years I'm projecting real growth." By ten years, this person could say, "I'm moving into a brand-new direction over the next 10 to 20 years, and I'm planning financially for my grandchildren and want to have everything in place for them."

Even later in this person's life, she could say, "I'm planning the direction of my company for 20 to 30 years, and this is where I'm taking it in the next decades to come." Finally, as this person matures and ages and becomes more sagelike and wise, with more of a universal perspective, she could be talking in terms of eternity instead of mortal times and spaces. At this stage, she patiently stays on course with her vision, and the fluctuations of daily or even yearly life cause little disturbance at all. As her vision, patience, and stability grow, so does her wealth.

A purpose is grander than a goal. Goals are necessary stages that you shed like booster rockets along the path of your purpose. The greater your purpose, the greater the power you can bring to bear upon your goals. A great purpose keeps your goals in perspective, and they seem much easier to achieve when measured against an immortal challenge.

Global Vision

When your financial purpose and dreams are focused on more than your immediate material needs, when they encompass the entire globe and all of humanity, a magical financial magnetism begins to emerge. Without a great purpose and vision, great events, accomplishments, and financial resources are unlikely to arise.

If you don't have a purpose greater than your physical life, you probably won't have any impact beyond it. If you'd love to make a difference in yourself, you'd better have a vision at least as big as your family. If you'd love to make a difference in your family, you'd better have a vision as big as your city. If you'd love to make a difference in your city, your vision must be as big as your state. If you'd love to make a difference in your state, you'd better have a vision as big as your nation. If you'd love to make a difference in your nation, you'd better have a vision as grand as the world. And if you'd love to have a global impact, you'd better have an immortal vision. Once your vision comes from a greater horizon, the impact of your product, service, or idea fills the realms below.

A chiropractor in Dallas heard me speak on this principle. He had a local practice that drew people within a ten-mile radius and that was about it. I said, "You can't make a difference anywhere unless you have a vision that comes from the level beyond," and he quickly grasped the idea. He began to affirm to himself, "My healing center is a beacon of light to the world."

I advised him to purchase a world globe on a stand and to mark his office on this globe and see it in relation to the rest of the world. I had him spin the globe around and imagine that people were coming to him from all over the world. Within a matter of *weeks,* he had people coming to him from around the state, from different states, and from *Asia,* just because he opened up his vision and receptivity.

I once asked a media mogul how he developed his international network. He said that at night he imagined himself holding a world globe with all the satellites around it, and he saw himself beaming selected information into whatever city on the planet he chose. He literally visualized himself standing in outer space, observing satellites around the earth, impacting the news systems around the world. As a result, he has created a global network system. Don't underestimate the power of vision. It's the source of mighty creations.

First visualize, then write down, your goals and purpose. Why? Because writing acts as the first step in taking things from the world of imagination to the physical world by defining them in space-time. Writing is a form of creation. It clarifies your mind, and when your mind is crystal clear on what it would love, it finds a way to manifest those goals. When you write your goals and purpose, you're also making a statement to the universe that you value manifesting them, and that helps motivate you as well. I write down exactly what I would love, and I become inspired by how it manifests.

I've had an affirmation for many years that helps me fulfill my vision. I say, "I'm the vision, God's the power, we're the team." (Or you could say the *universe* is the power, if you prefer.) When I say this affirmation, I truly feel that I have the power to overcome any obstacles in the way of my dreams. If I keep my end of the bargain by maintaining the vision, the Ultimate Source seems to provide all the required power. It's vital to tap in to the core deep inside yourself that knows you have a destiny, where a force much greater than your brain inspires you to fulfill it. The magnitude of your cause determines the magnitude of your resources and influence. They're directly proportionate to the sphere of consciousness with which you resonate.

> *"Your vision will become clear only*
> *when you can look into your own heart.*
> *Who looks outside, dreams; who looks inside, awakes."*

> — Carl Jung

A Cause

You are a soul whose true nature is light, on a journey to ever-higher levels of consciousness and states of divine expression. Your vitality on that journey is directly proportionate to the vividness of your vision. If you don't have something challenging and fulfilling to awaken for in the morning, you won't *rise* and *shine.* Unless your goals are vast and growing, you'll tend to slow down as you approach their fulfillment rather than letting yourself run out of things to do. In other words, you won't let yourself become extinct. That's why it's important to keep clarifying your purpose and expanding your goals and heavenly dreams.

Even with a clear purpose, you'll occasionally be distracted and uninspired. The only reason you're not inspired at those times is because you haven't linked what you're doing to your purpose. Make a list of everything you do in a normal day and ask yourself, "How does that help me fulfill my mission?" Keep linking everything to what you'd love, and find its meaning and significance in your life. Anything you don't see as part of your purpose feels pointless, and the ratio of pointlessness to purposefulness is how much hell or heaven you have in your life. Ask that question, and keep asking and linking until it doesn't matter *what* you do, you feel you're on purpose. The truth is that everything you do is connected, and the more you link your actions to your purpose, the more you get to do what you love.

Here's another reason to keep growing your vision. If you only have a dollar and you earn another, the second dollar is worth 100 percent of the first one's value. If you have $10 and earn a dollar, it's only worth 10 percent of the value to you. If you have $100, a dollar is worth 1 percent, if you have $1,000 it's worth 0.1 percent, and if you have $10,000 it's only worth 0.01 percent. Get the message? The first dollar has a high value, but as your wealth increases, each additional dollar has less and less value. Therefore, if your only purpose for having money is the money itself, you'll diminish the desire to earn more as you accumulate it. The value of each dollar decreases to the point where making money no longer has the power to motivate you. So here's the law: If your purpose for making money doesn't grow at a faster rate than it depreciates in value to you, you'll eventually plateau, and either stop attracting wealth or squander it on low priorities.

Money flees from those who have no purpose for it,
and flows to those who do.

The Salesman

A gentleman came to see me and said, "I want to boost my multilevel marketing and network business."

I asked him, "Why do you want to do that?"

"Because I want to make more money."

"You don't move me with that," I said. *"Why* do you want to make more money?"

"Well, I just do."

"That won't cut it. What's your reason?"

"Uh, I want to put my kids through college."

"Are you on track for that?"

"Yes, I am."

"So what's your next cause? If sending your kids to college is your only cause, you won't attract money beyond it. You want to make more money, yet you don't have a vision to do anything *with* it. The universe meets you halfway. It doesn't give you what you're not willing meet with a cause. So what are you going to do with this wealth? If you died tomorrow, what's incomplete in your life? What's left undone?"

He looked over at his wife and said, "Well, uh . . ." He felt guilty because he knew his dreams but he wasn't sure she'd approve. He was denying himself his purpose for fear of what someone else thought, so I pushed him a little and he finally blurted out, "What I'd really love to do is fulfill my dream of donating $1 million to my church. I've only given about $20,000 so far."

"Great, write it down. What else?"

"My wife and I would love to travel around the world first class."

"Great. What else would you love to do?"

"I'd love to buy each of my children a car when they graduate."

We kept going, and I had him list 40 things he'd love to do. I helped him structure and organize them, and out of that came a whole list of other dreams and details that he'd buried. They'd been waiting inside his heart and mind the whole time, and he really had a huge drive to do them, but he hadn't brought them to the surface and focused on them. Now he had urgency and a reason to grow. He had something beyond himself to live for, and his business went to levels he couldn't even imagine before. If he hadn't grown his vision, not only would his business have stayed stagnant, he might have *died* putting his kids through school, because he had nothing left to accomplish.

Hit Men Again

As you follow the principles in this book and your money increases, one day you'll no longer "have to" work, but you'll still love to serve. At that point, you'll still require a cause to keep growing and remain inspired by life.

The financiers who opened their hearts to the man they were considering having killed came to me about six months later with another issue. They said, "That work we did with you made a huge impact on our lives and made us a lot of money, but now we want to go to another level in our thinking. Can you do anything that will lift our operation and give us access to even wealthier people and more finances?"

I said, "You won't go to a greater level without a greater cause, so what's your cause?"

"We want to get involved in international real estate."

"And that's inspiring to you?"

"Uh, no, not really."

"You can't get beyond yourself until you have a cause that's greater than you," I said. "What vision brings tears of inspiration to your eyes?" I helped them look back over their lives at what had deeply moved them until one of them contacted a very deep cause. As a child, he'd lived in London in great poverty, but his street was the dividing line between the rich and the poor in that area. Even though he was impoverished, he'd gone to school with the wealthy children, and he'd felt utterly humiliated for years because he came from the wrong side of the street. I showed him how that experience was possibly the source of his driving force to become wealthy and accomplish many of his achievements. He became grateful for it, and now they had a vast cause: to set up educational and philanthropic systems in selected countries in the world that would break down some of the barriers between rich and poor.

They moved to another level with that cause, and their income and outreach increased almost immediately. Why? Because people are drawn to, and invest in, inspiration more than desperation and great causes more than little ones.

If someone said to you, "Look, I'm having financial problems, and I need $5,000 to pay some bills, could you help me out?" You'd probably say, "No, thank you! Take care of your own life." But what if someone said, "Excuse me. I have three children. My husband just passed away and I've been out of the workforce since my first child was born. I don't want something for nothing, but we truly need help. I'll sign a contract, pay you fair interest, and guarantee the loan." You'd be more apt to respond because there's more integrity, and it's not just an individual, but also a family.

If someone said, "They've found that playing in nature reduces crime and drug use by city kids, and this poor neighborhood is without parks. I've bought two properties with my own money, and I'm raising more to landscape it and buy safe equipment for the kids to play on. Would you like to help me create that for these children?" it moves the cause up to a community level, and your willingness to contribute is greater again.

And what about, "Our daughter was born with a brain disorder that causes learning disabilities and hyperactivity in a growing percentage of children. My wife and I used our life savings to set up a research and educational foundation, and we'd love to have any donation to help our cause. Our vision is not only to help these children learn, but to help all children discover their talents. We're doing this on a statewide basis, and eventually we plan to help children all across the country."

The bigger and more inspiring your cause, the more people and money are drawn in to help you achieve it. You can't receive an inspiring idea without also having the capacity to make that idea come true and become handsomely paid for it. You just wouldn't resonate with it otherwise. The quality of your life is based upon the quality of the questions you ask, and if you can see the life you'd love to live, you can ask the questions to make it happen. Ask yourself, "How do I do what I love and get greatly paid for it?" and don't stop asking the question until you receive the answer.

> *"You are never given a wish without also*
> *being given the power to make it come true.*
> *You may have to work for it, however."*
>
> — Richard Bach

The Vision

Don't underestimate the power of inspired, soul-directed vision; it's the most powerful resource you have access to. If you practice and refine your ability to tune in to your vision, "impossible" things can happen.

During the time of my first practice, in my daily meditation at my home I received one of the strongest revelations of my life. I had an absolutely vivid, clear-as-crystal vision of my new office. It was in a building called the Transco Tower. In my vision, I stood hundreds of feet in the air, looking out over the city. I saw the layout of the rooms, saw the floor number (52), and heard a voice saying that this was my space. I'd just expanded, signed a lease, and spent a lot of money at my first office, so it seemed absurd to move. But I've learned over the years not to ignore inspiring messages like that. When the voice truly speaks to you, it's wise to listen.

That afternoon I went back and told the doctors working for me that they had until the end of the week to decide whether they wanted to buy my practice or I'd put it on the market. That was a Tuesday, and on Thursday morning I drove to the Transco Tower and spoke to the leasing agent.

I said, "I'm a chiropractor, and I'd love to lease an office in your building."

She said, "Well, I can tell you right now that's not possible. All of our companies specialize in energy, oil, and money."

I responded, "Ma'am, I'm as slick as oil, I have *unbelievable* amounts of energy, and I've got lots of money. I'd fit right in here."

She looked at me sternly: "I don't think you understand, *sir.* There never have been and won't be any doctors here. We don't want the clinical liabilities. Unless you have an oil or energy company or are involved in banking, legalities, or investing, there's no place available here."

"Well, if there were any spaces available, which floor would they be on?"

"We're almost fully occupied, except for a space on floor 52."

"Perfect," I said. "You don't mind if I just see it, do you? If I must start up another company just to fit in, then so be it. But you see, I had a vision about this place." So I talked her into taking me up to floor 52. I walked in and stood in the corner of the building and looked out; I was up almost 600 feet looking out, and I couldn't help it, I just started to cry. I'd never been in that building before, but I saw the exact view I'd seen in my head two days before. When you get proof like that of a spiritual vision and powers beyond the normal world, your heart just opens up.

The leasing agent was standing over by the door in her impatience to get rid of me, but when I turned around to face her and she saw the tears running down my face, she asked, "Are you okay?"

Quietly I said, "This is my space. I saw this exact place in my head two days ago. I'm destined to be here, and I don't think anything's going to be able to stop it. My purpose and vision are lining up. This is it."

She really looked at me then, resisting tears herself because I was so openhearted, and she said, "You're serious, aren't you?"

I said, "Absolutely."

"You know," she replied, "I'm beginning to believe you."

"I'm serious. I'll meet with the owner if necessary. I'll do whatever it takes to be here."

"Well, I've never met anybody like you," she said. "This is new to me. They've never let a doctor in, but I'll do what I can."

While she went to her office to make some calls, I went into the architect's office next door. I said, "Hi, I'm Dr. Demartini. Do you have the floor plans for floor 52? I'm going to be a new tenant there, and I'd love to start designing my space." I drew the entire floor plan the way I'd envisioned it and handed it to him, saying, "They're making special arrangements for me, so if you could begin your designs, we'll get started right away."

When the leasing agent returned, she said, "I can't guarantee you'll get in, but I can't say you won't. They want three years of tax returns, your company mission statement, your profit-and-loss sheets with all your financials and liabilities. They want to know the details and objectives of your practice . . ." and on and on. That was before they'd even consider me, but I was back the next Tuesday with it all packaged in a folder marked DEMARTINI, and one of my earlier books on top.

Two days later, the leasing agent called my office and said, "Dr. Demartini, welcome to Transco Tower. You're the only doctor who's ever been able to pass through the system." Twenty-seven days after I signed the lease; the office was built to perfection.

I sold my other practice at the end of that month, moved in, and began the elevator seminars soon after. That office was a pivotal place for me, a whole new resonance. It advanced my career and wealth. And to this day, 17 years later, I'm still the only doctor in that building. The universe just came in and shifted everything around because I was willing to listen to and act on what my inner voice told me.

Every goal requires support and challenge, but most people give up the moment that things get tough. When they feel challenged, they say, "Well, it must not have been meant to be." Challenge is the barrier that must be overcome before you can grow to the next level. If it were easy, everyone would do it. There's a selection process going on, and those who are willing to pay the price and face their fears get the rewards. A great purpose gives you the courage to transcend your own limitations and achieve great and heavenly riches.

> *"It is funny about life. If you refuse to accept anything but the very best, you will very often get it."*
>
> — W. Somerset Maugham

The Actress

I once sat next to a young lady on a flight from Houston to New York who drew my attention by wearing dark glasses inside the plane at night and acting very aloof. At first she thought I was after an interview or an autograph, but when I reassured her that I was simply interested in studying people, she admitted that she was an actress. Then she turned away to look out the window.

I asked her, "So what made you become an actress?" and suddenly she turned back to me with her eyes shining.

She said, "When I was three years old, my mother took me to see Judy Garland onstage, and when I saw her singing and dancing I said to myself, *That's my destiny. Someday I'm going to do that.*" Her mother realized how enraptured she was and enrolled her in singing, dancing, and drama classes soon afterward. When the purpose awoke in her heart, the necessary support and challenges appeared to help her fulfill it.

I asked, "Do you focus your mind on this dream?"

"Oh, yes. I was born to be an actress, and it's *all* I think about. I think about my next role, my next interview or movie. I think about the actors and directors I want to work with, and I see myself receiving awards. I think about it every day."

"Do you say any affirmations to yourself?" She quickly pulled out a little dog-eared piece of paper and showed me her affirmation, which simply said, "I sing. I dance." Ever since she was a tiny child, she'd been looking at that piece of paper and never losing sight of her dream. The power of those simple words was tremendous.

When you receive *your* inspiring message that clearly, when you see the details of your dream that vividly and affirm and visualize and commit yourself to it until tears come to your eyes and nothing in this world will keep you from it, that's your destiny. Clarifying your purpose is one of the most important acts of your life. It's your direction, your meaning, your *why* for existence. With greater meaning, you'll have more gratitude and love for life, and you'll manifest a greater *life*. If you don't know exactly what you'd do with $1 million, why would the universe give it to you? If you don't know what you'd love to do with your life, why would the universe give you more life? So from now on, whenever you hear yourself saying, "I don't know my purpose," turn it around and say, "I *know* my purpose, I *live* my purpose, I *love* my purpose," and it will be revealed to you in ever greater detail and clarity.

> *"What our deepest self craves is not mere enjoyment,*
> *but some supreme purpose that will enlist all our powers and*
> *give unity and direction to our life."*
>
> — Henry J. Golding

Fulfill What You Love

According to traditional beliefs, the only way to be kept out of heaven is to commit a mortal sin, to break God's law. Have you learned one thing in this book that could earn the eternal wrath of an all-wise, all-loving Creator? How could honoring yourself, maintaining fair exchange in all your affairs, being grateful for everything you receive, allowing yourself to experience the finest this world has to offer, turning emotions into love, and listening to your soul and obeying be anything but God's law? Desperate people do desperate things, while inspired people do inspired things. Making a hell of a profit is far more likely to cause you to act in inspiring and heavenly ways than not.

You're not a finite little being having occasional glimpses of spirit. You're a spiritual being of an infinite nature having a temporary mortal experience. You have purpose in your soul, just as you have love in your heart. And when you're inspired and purposeful, you grow, because you're investing in your soul. Those who don't honor themselves by fulfilling their purpose of inspiration and evolution automatically break down their body and dissipate their wealth. Their resources are given to those who *are* following their mission. The purpose of evolution is to grow consciousness, and that's how it works. To those who have, more is given; to those who have not, more is taken away.

No matter what you do, your role is to be inspired. Anytime you're not inspired about your life, wealth and opportunities flow away from you because you're ignoring the universal imperative to *live your soul's dreams and make them real.* When people feel that the world is unjust because others are being given everything and they're receiving nothing, it's only because they're not living their dreams. They're perfectly capable of doing so, but they have yet to listen to their inner voice, which always says, "Fulfill what you love."

A person with a mission has a message, and when you find that message, your business, your wealth, and your life will boom. When you can't wait to share your message with people, they can't wait to hear you. You'll face trials and tribulations along the road to your dreams, but what else will you do with your life? Unless you work on what's in your heart, you'll break it. Don't let anything on the inside or the outside keep you from your dream, because your dream *is* your life—your spiritual calling brought into physical reality. The higher the calling, the greater the worldly rewards for bringing it here. That dream is heaven for you, and it's here now.

Exercise 1

Choose a quiet time when you won't be interrupted, and begin inwardly giving thanks for everything in your life for which you're deeply grateful. Thank God for your wife or husband, your children, and your friends. Keep going until you feel your heart open and you get a tear in your eye. It's easier than you might think.

The minute you get that feeling, address your Source and say, "What would you love me to fulfill? What's my purpose here on Earth?" You can call this highest inner source of being whatever moves you most—the Source, God, or your soul—but *ask* it what it wants you to do. I say, "Dear God, I ask that I may be worthy of receiving your divine revelation, that I may be receptive to your grace. I ask that my heart be opened and the outlines of my destiny be revealed, that I may be humbled to the truth you provide before me."

Thank your Source in advance for its wisdom.

If you're truly grateful, the message will come at the speed of light, so get ready to write it down. If it doesn't come instantly, simply think more deeply about what you're grateful for and ask again.

Write all your messages down, and ask your Source for further instructions before you act: "Thank you for this insight. Can you give me more details? Is there a time when I am to do this?" Don't be afraid to ask questions of your Inner Guidance. Listening to and trusting your inner voice is one of the greatest resources on Earth. It's pure wisdom, and all the great leaders have mastered it. Geniuses are those who listen to their inner message, see their soul's inner vision, and obey. The light of the soul is wisdom.

Exercise 2

When you have a glimpse of your purpose, the next challenge is to manifest it. Every morning, write down the seven highest priority action steps you *know* you can take to help you fulfill your dreams and purpose. Schedule your day to give priority to what's most important to you. Do this every day for a month and you'll begin to see a pattern.

That pattern is the secret to becoming most effective and efficient at what you'd love to do. I did this for two years and found that there are four things I do most powerfully: research, write, travel, and speak. Now that's basically *all* I do; everything else is delegated. When I do those four things, my dreams manifest.

Once you find your four highest priority actions and stick to them, the rest of your life seems to fall into place because you attract the resources to take care of all your other values. People who focus on their top priorities grow in self-worth, wealth, and outreach, so discipline yourself and grow.

Words of Wisdom and Power

- *My why is so big that the hows take care of themselves.*

- *I know my purpose, I live my purpose, I love my purpose.*

- *How is <u>this</u> connected to my purpose?*

- *I have a global vision, and the world rewards me for it.*

- *God is the power, I am the vision, and we are the team.*

- *My soul speaks to me with great wisdom.*
  I listen and obey.

Afterword

THANK YOU for coming on this journey with me. I hope these stories and principles have touched your heart, inspired your mind, and moved you to fashion your heavenly life in the image of your highest vision. I hope we may meet someday and you can say to me, "Dr. Demartini, I followed your advice, and it transformed my life. I have great wealth, I have the life I dreamed of, and I have a purpose that brings tears to my eyes and inspires me every day to become something greater."

One day you'll know, but until then, dream and act. Thank you.

May you make one hell of a profit and still get to heaven!

— **Dr. John F. Demartini**

Acknowledgments

To Tim Marlowe, for his assistance in the compilation and editing of the initial manuscript.

To Reid Tracy, (president/CEO) and Jill Kramer (editorial director) of Hay House, and to freelance editor Gail Fink, for making this book possible through their specialized expertise, guidance, and sound advice.

About the Author

Dr. John F. Demartini is a professional speaker, author, and business consultant whose clients range from Wall Street financiers, financial planners, and corporate executives to health-care professionals, actors, and sports personalities.

The author of *The Breakthrough Experience* and founder of the Concourse of Wisdom School of Philosophy and Healing, Dr. Demartini is a rare and gifted man whose span of experience and study encompasses broad scopes of knowledge. He began his career as a doctor of chiropractic and went on to explore more than 200 different disciplines in pursuit of what he calls Universal Principles of Life and Health. As an international speaker, Dr. Demartini breathes new life into his audiences with his enlightening perspectives, humorous observations of human nature, and practical action steps. His words of wisdom inspire minds, open hearts, and motivate people into action. His philosophy and revolutionary understanding of the power of unconditional love is are changing the lives of millions of people all over the world.

If you'd like information on attending *The Breakthrough Experience*™ or consulting with Dr. Demartini to experience *The Quantum Collapse Process*™, contact Dr. Demartini's Concourse of Wisdom Headquarters at:

Dr. John F. Demartini
2800 Post Oak Blvd., #5250
Houston, TX 77056

Toll-free: 888–DEMARTINI
Phone: 713–850–1234
Fax: 713–850–9239
www.drdemartini.com
info@drdemartini.com

NOTES

NOTES

NOTES

NOTES

NOTES

NOTES

NOTES

NOTES

NOTES

NOTES

NOTES

We hope you enjoyed this Hay House book.
If you'd like to receive our online catalog featuring additional
information on Hay House books and products, or if you'd like
to find out more about the Hay Foundation, please contact:

Hay House, Inc.
P.O. Box 5100
Carlsbad, CA 92018-5100

(760) 431-7695 or (800) 654-5126
(760) 431-6948 (fax) or (800) 650-5115 (fax)
www.hayhouse.com® • www.hayfoundation.org

Published and distributed in Australia by: Hay House Australia Pty. Ltd.,
18/36 Ralph St., Alexandria NSW 2015 • *Phone:* 612-9669-4299
Fax: 612-9669-4144 • www.hayhouse.com.au

Published and distributed in the United Kingdom by: Hay House UK, Ltd.,
292B Kensal Rd., London W10 5BE • *Phone:* 44-20-8962-1230
Fax: 44-20-8962-1239 • www.hayhouse.co.uk

Published and distributed in the Republic of South Africa by: Hay House SA (Pty),
Ltd., P.O. Box 990, Witkoppen 2068 • *Phone/Fax:* 27-11-467-8904
www.hayhouse.co.za

Published in India by: Hay House Publishers India, Muskaan Complex, Plot No. 3,
B-2, Vasant Kunj, New Delhi 110 070 • *Phone:* 91-11-4176-1620
Fax: 91-11-4176-1630 • www.hayhouse.co.in

Distributed in Canada by: Raincoast, 9050 Shaughnessy St., Vancouver, B.C. V6P
6E5 *Phone:* (604) 323-7100 • *Fax:* (604) 323-2600 • www.raincoast.com

Take Your Soul on a Vacation

Visit **www.HealYourLife.com®** to regroup, recharge, and reconnect
with your own magnificence.Featuring blogs, mind-body-spirit news,
and life-changing wisdom from Louise Hay and friends.

Visit **www.HealYourLife.com** today!